COUNTRY MUSIC HALL OF FAME®
AND MUSEUM

HONOR THY MUSIC®

Country Music Foundation Press • 222 Fifth Avenue South • Nashville, Tennessee 37203

Editor: Michael McCall   Designer: Margaret Pesek

The artifacts, documents, and photographs contained in this book come from the collection of the Country Music Hall of Fame® and Museum.

This project reflects the work of many Country Music Hall of Fame and Museum staff members.
Although space prohibits listing them all, the contributions of Director Kyle Young; Vice President, Museum Services Carolyn Tate; Vice President, Museum Programs Jay Orr; Vice President, Sales and Marketing Sharon Burns; Senior Historian John Rumble; Photo Collection Manager Tim Davis; Creative Director Warren Denney; and designer Adrianne Murray deserve special mention.

Photographers Bob Delevante, Marty Stuart, Les Leverett, Donn Jones, and david w. clements deserve recognition for their contributions to this book.

CONTENTS

Background: Detail of stage jacket made for Buck Owens by Nudie the Rodeo Tailor.

INTRODUCTION

The Country Music Hall of Fame® and Museum is the world's largest repository of country music artifacts and one if its largest music research centers. The crown jewels of this vast collection are presented through dynamic, colorful exhibits featuring one-of-a-kind artifacts and a treasure trove of historic recordings, films, and videos.

The museum's permanent exhibit, *Sing Me Back Home: A Journey Through Country Music*, is divided into two sections: *Sing Me Back Home: The Journey Begins* traces country music from its humble folk roots through its exciting evolution into an internationally recognized commercial art form. *Dreaming My Dreams: The Journey Continues* carries the music forward from the 1960s to the artists of today.

The Country Music Hall of Fame and Museum opened on April 1, 1967, at the head of Music Row. In May 2001, the museum moved to a 140,000-square-foot facility in downtown Nashville. Within ten years, it became clear the museum needed more space, based on continuing growth and popularity, leading to an expansion to a total of 350,000 square feet, situated on a central downtown campus including the Music City Convention Center and Omni Nashville Hotel.

The museum operates Historic RCA Studio B in partnership with the Mike Curb Family Foundation. The museum also owns Hatch Show Print, the oldest active poster print shop in America. Other museum offerings include a full menu of live performances and public programs, shopping in the Museum Store, dining at the Two Twenty-Two Grill and Catering, and hosting events in the building's many fabulous public spaces—all contributing to an unforgettable museum experience.

Tuxedo jacket, shirt, and bowtie worn by Jim Reeves.

Western shirt made for Tex Ritter by Nathan Turk, and cowboy hat inscribed from Ritter to Webb Pierce and his wife Audrey.

THE ARCHITECTURE

THE MUSEUM BUILDING

The Country Music Hall of Fame and Museum's acclaimed building celebrates country music's origins and inspirations through many architectural details.

Viewed from above, the building's outline resembles a massive bass clef. The vertical windows in front are positioned like the black and white keys of a piano, and the dramatic sweep of the building's concrete roofline recalls the tail fin of a late 1950s Cadillac. A replica of the iconic WSM radio tower pierces the roof of the Hall of Fame Rotunda, also evoking a church steeple.

The Hall of Fame Rotunda, with its cylindrical shape, references small-town water towers and grain silos. It is topped by four concentric circles that represent the 78-, 45-, and 33-rpm vinyl records and the compact disc. Stone bars on the outside of the Rotunda symbolize the musical notes of the classic Carter Family song "Will the Circle Be Unbroken."

Inside, the Conservatory entrance, bathed in natural light, features a steel frame inspired by the railroads and bridges connecting small-town America. A stream flowing from the second floor to a fountain in the Conservatory represents the movement of music across the American landscape. The floor consists of blocks of southern yellow pine, used in factories and warehouses. Walls of crab orchard stone, from East Tennessee, lend a rustic touch.

All together, the building provides a welcoming yet dignified home for preserving and presenting country music history.

SING ME BACK HOME:
THE JOURNEY BEGINS

The museum's permanent exhibit begins with *Sing Me Back Home*, a vibrant, multifaceted journey through the first four decades of country music. The exhibit cases illustrate the depth of the museum's archival collection, with one-of-a-kind artifacts collected from the artists who made country music such an integral part of American culture.

Adding to the experience, the museum presents historic photographs, original recordings, archival video and film, interactive media, and beautifully rendered text panels. *Sing Me Back Home* immerses visitors in the history, sights, and sounds of country music through the lives and voices of many of its most beloved personalities.

Custom western-style boots worn by Roy Rogers.

DeFord Bailey

Bradley Kincaid

THE DAWN OF COUNTRY MUSIC

Country music's roots reach into the beginnings of American history. Settlers brought music with them as they explored the New World, and various strains coalesced to form what came to be known as country music.

As a commercial art form, country music didn't exist until the early twentieth century, when the advent of phonographs and radios allowed vernacular music to be recorded, sold, and broadcast widely. With Thomas Edison's invention of the phonograph in 1877, what started out as the "talking machine" soon became a popular means for musical performances to be captured and eventually packaged and marketed. Sales grew in the early 1900s, after recordings evolved from cylinders to discs. By the 1920s, companies such as Columbia

Harmonica and megaphone used by DeFord Bailey.

Banner promoting Blue Sky Boys performances on radio station WGST, Atlanta.

Left to right: Jimmie Rodgers with the Carter Family: Maybelle Carter, A.P. Carter, Sara Carter, 1931.

Jimmie Rodgers's brakeman's cap and guitar.

Records and the Victor Talking Machine Company found that recordings with regional sounds and themes became favorites among buyers, and executives at the record companies began traveling the rural South to find homegrown performers.

Radio stations proliferated across America after 1920, becoming a major outlet for musical performances. As with recordings, music with rustic overtones proved popular on the airwaves. Country musicians first performed on radio in 1922, and the following year, radio station WBAP in Forth Worth, Texas, initiated the first barn dance—an ensemble variety program with the relaxed, chatty atmosphere of a family gathering. Such down-home shows drew in rural audiences as well as city dwellers attracted to the old-fashioned way of life the barn-dance programs recalled.

Left: Pop Stoneman's autoharp, with carrying case designed to act as an amplifier when the autoharp was placed on the lid.

Right: Fiddle used by Fiddlin' John Carson, and handpainted acoustic guitar played by his daughter and performance partner, Moonshine Kate.

Pop Stoneman

Blue Sky Boys

Radio stations in Chicago, Nashville, and other cities soon launched their own barn dances, attracting loyal fans and advertisers. Regional and national businesses, eager to associate their products with the traditional themes of these shows, lined up to sign on as sponsors. Thanks to the spread of rustic programs, country entertainers got more work and greater exposure, making them a vital part of listeners' lives.

Audience members attached themselves to favorite performers, and the first country stars emerged, including Jimmie Rodgers, the Carter Family, Uncle Dave Macon, and Vernon Dalhart.

Through the twentieth century, even as technologies changed, country music would continue to find favor with the public via recordings and radio airplay—much as it had in its very earliest days.

Mandolin and guitar used by the Blue Sky Boys.

Bonnie Dodd

Fiddlin' John Carson and Moonshine Kate

Paul Warmack's Gully Jumpers

Left: Bonnie Dodd's National resonator guitar.   Right: Bradley Kincaid's guitar.

STEEL GUITAR RAG:

STYLISTIC INNOVATIONS

Country music in the 1920s and 1930s benefited from an exciting infusion of regional diversity. Country's principal sound remained that of fiddle-driven stringbands, but some groups began incorporating pop and jazz influences that broadened the music's possibilities.

In Chicago, the Prairie Ramblers (which included singer Patsy Montana) injected swing and cowboy music into their repertoire while dressing in western outfits.

In the Southwest, fiddle-band veterans such as Milton Brown drew inspiration from jazz and blues to create western swing. In Louisiana, the Hackberry Ramblers merged Cajun fiddle music with country music, eventually growing into a full-fledged Louisiana swing band, complete with horns and drums.

The Hackberry Ramblers

Milton Brown & His Musical Brownies

Guitar and custom-painted drum played by members of the Hackberry Ramblers.

Meanwhile, improvements in microphones and recording techniques allowed the subtle harmonies of country duet acts to emerge as a creative force. The Blue Sky Boys and the Delmore Brothers set standards for how sweetly powerful two male voices could sound. Other important duos included the Callahan Brothers, the Carlisle Brothers, Karl & Harty, Lulu Belle & Scotty, and the Monroe Brothers.

As these stylistic adaptations suggested, country music would be a flexible, evolving musical form that embraced new sounds while remaining rooted in traditions.

Left: Tenor banjo played by Chick Hurt of the Prairie Ramblers.

Right: Western boots worn by Chick Hurt of the Prairie Ramblers.

Far Right: Lap steel used by Bob Dunn of the Milton Brown & His Musical Brownies.

Prairie Ramblers with Patsy Montana

Delmore Brothers

Carl T. Sprague

Patsy Montana

BACK IN THE SADDLE:
THE WESTERN INFLUENCE

In American mythology, the cowboy represents bravery, romance, and self-sufficiency. No wonder that musically diverse country entertainers, seeking a visual style that spoke of heartland values, adopted the western look.

Jimmie Rodgers, one of country music's first national stars, sometimes wore broad-brimmed cowboy hats and leather chaps for publicity photos. Rodgers acolytes Ernest Tubb, Hank Williams, and Hank Snow would adopt their own versions of western costuming.

In the 1930s, Carl T. Sprague recorded authentic western songs he learned while herding cattle in Texas. Around the same time, Gene Autry became a star on Chicago radio station WLS before moving to

Left: Detail of artwork on the back of Carl T. Sprague's resonator guitar.

Right: Patsy Montana's western boots, which she designed.

Below: Tex Ritter's Colt single-action revolver.

Gene Autry *Roy Rogers* *Tex Ritter*

Los Angeles in 1934. His appearance in the 1934 Republic Pictures film *In Old Santa Fe* launched one of the era's most successful film-acting careers; the down-home warmth of Autry's baritone voice and the humble heroism of his screen character proved reassuring to Depression Era audiences.

Tex Ritter, another Lone Star native, played cowboys in Broadway musicals and on radio shows before starring in his first western film in 1936. In the 1940s, Roy Rogers emerged as the most successful film cowboy since Autry. Born Leonard Slye, Rogers was given his screen name by Hollywood. In 1947, he married his most popular co-star, Dale Evans, and the two later starred in a TV series, *The Roy Rogers Show.*

Marty Robbins, Willie Nelson, George Strait, and Garth Brooks are among other stars who have shown a cowboy influence. Like a good country song, the western look is intrinsically American—and suggests that certain values remain strong no matter what else is going on in the world.

Top right: Poster promoting Trail to San Antone, *starring Gene Autry.*

Right: Dale Evans's boots, and plastic figurine of Roy Rogers on his horse, Trigger.

Detail of accordion played by Pee Wee King.

TENNESSEE SATURDAY NIGHT:
NASHVILLE TAKES THE LEAD

By the 1940s, Nashville was fast becoming the capital of country music. The Grand Ole Opry gained in national prominence when the NBC Radio Network began broadcasting a half hour of the program on Saturday evenings in October 1939. By the mid–1940s, this popular segment, sponsored by Prince Albert Smoking Tobacco, helped transform the Opry from one of many regionally popular barn dances into a nationally known radio program with a reputation for developing country music stars.

In 1943, the Opry's popularity led to a move to the Ryman Auditorium on Fifth Avenue in downtown Nashville, allowing for larger audiences at its live weekly program. Each Saturday night, the Ryman hosted two audiences of some 2,000 persons, many of whom came from different states.

Minnie Pearl

Pee Wee King's accordion.

Roy Acuff's fiddle.

Roy Acuff

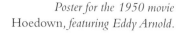

Poster for the 1950 movie
Hoedown, *featuring Eddy Arnold.*

Dress and hat worn by Minnie Pearl for her first
appearance on the Grand Ole Opry in 1940.

The Opry cast members who became national stars in the 1940s included Roy Acuff, Eddy Arnold, Red Foley, Pee Wee King, Bill Monroe, Minnie Pearl, and Ernest Tubb. As more stars emerged from Nashville, the city began growing into a recording and music-business center.

Acuff and songwriter Fred Rose formed the music publishing firm Acuff-Rose Publications in 1942, making it one of the first prominent music companies in town. Two years later, Eddy Arnold successfully cut a hit record in Nashville, and subsequently the city's reputation as a recording hub grew, drawing more attention and investment from major record labels headquartered in New York.

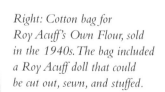

Right: Cotton bag for Roy Acuff's Own Flour, sold in the 1940s. The bag included a Roy Acuff doll that could be cut out, sewn, and stuffed.

Left: Eddy Arnold's 1967 Gibson J-200N guitar, an almost exact reproduction of his 1948 guitar of the same model.

*Hank Williams's suit, made
by Nudie the Rodeo Tailor.*

In 1946, Fred Rose began working with Hank Williams, then a young, little-known songwriter and performer residing in Montgomery, Alabama. By 1947, Rose had secured Williams a record contract and had begun producing his recordings. Two years later, when Williams achieved his first #1 hit, "Lovesick Blues," the lanky Alabama singer left the *Louisiana Hayride* barn dance in Shreveport to accept an invitation to join the Grand Ole Opry, moving to Nashville with his wife and newborn boy.

The national impact Williams had as a recording artist and a touring member of the Opry heightened the prominence of the radio show and Nashville as the place many aspiring country artists, musicians, and songwriters wanted to be. Soon, the music industry bloomed around all the talent moving to Middle Tennessee.

Pee Wee King

Eddy Arnold

Hank Williams

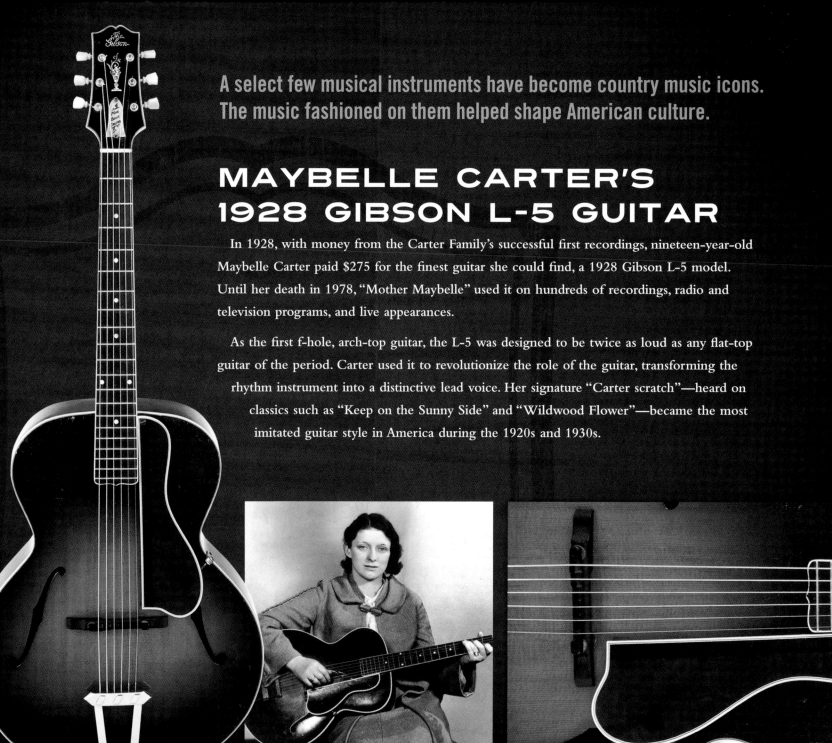

THE PRECIOUS JEWEL

A select few musical instruments have become country music icons. The music fashioned on them helped shape American culture.

MAYBELLE CARTER'S 1928 GIBSON L-5 GUITAR

In 1928, with money from the Carter Family's successful first recordings, nineteen-year-old Maybelle Carter paid $275 for the finest guitar she could find, a 1928 Gibson L-5 model. Until her death in 1978, "Mother Maybelle" used it on hundreds of recordings, radio and television programs, and live appearances.

As the first f-hole, arch-top guitar, the L-5 was designed to be twice as loud as any flat-top guitar of the period. Carter used it to revolutionize the role of the guitar, transforming the rhythm instrument into a distinctive lead voice. Her signature "Carter scratch"—heard on classics such as "Keep on the Sunny Side" and "Wildwood Flower"—became the most imitated guitar style in America during the 1920s and 1930s.

These treasures are currently displayed as part of the museum's collection—and serve as enduring symbols of the power of music.

BILL MONROE'S
1923 GIBSON F-5 MANDOLIN

The most famous mandolin in American music history, Bill Monroe's Gibson F-5 Master Model is one of the finest stringed instruments ever made.

Monroe bought the instrument in the early 1940s, when he spotted it in a Florida barbershop window. It became his second voice, filling in around his high, lonesome singing, and ringing out during the supercharged solos that were a hallmark of his aggressive playing style.

In 1985, an intruder broke into Monroe's home and smashed the treasured mandolin with a fireplace poker. The instrument was painstakingly reconstructed by Gibson from about 150 slivers of broken wood, and it remained Monroe's constant companion, onstage and in the recording studio, for the rest of his life.

Detail of Cindy Walker's Royal typewriter.

Words and Music
CINDY WALKER

HOLLYWOOD BARN DANCE:

COUNTRY MOVES WEST

Among the Dust Bowl images imprinted on history are cars full of rural migrants crammed with family belongings. Often, the baggage included a musical instrument—a visual reminder that those on the move carried their music with them to California.

Indeed, Los Angeles, Bakersfield, and other California cities became country music outposts largely because working-class Americans brought in honky-tonk, western swing, and other country styles. Soon, country sounds filled dance halls, radio programs, and recording studios, and performers like Bob Wills & His Texas Playboys, Spade Cooley, Hank Thompson, and Merle Travis went there to advance their legendary careers.

Right: Custom-painted Royal typewriter used by Cindy Walker to compose her hit songs.

Below: Bob Wills's inlaid fiddle.

Cindy Walker

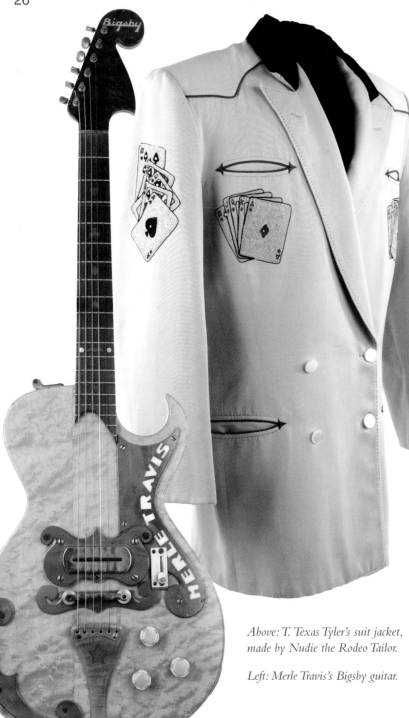

Merle Travis

T. Texas Tyler

Above: T. Texas Tyler's suit jacket, made by Nudie the Rodeo Tailor.

Left: Merle Travis's Bigsby guitar.

From Long Beach in the south to Oakland in the north—two cities that lured workers to defense-industry jobs—western swing bands led by Wills and Cooley attracted crowds competing in number with those of swing-era giants Tommy Dorsey and Benny Goodman.

Wills already was a star in Texas and Oklahoma when, in 1943, he returned from military service in World War II and relocated his band, the Texas Playboys, from Tulsa to Los Angeles. The charismatic, cigar-chomping fiddler proved his instincts were right, as he became one of the nation's highest-paid bandleaders. Wills also recorded some of his best-loved hits during this period, including "Texas Playboy Rag" (1945). Like Wills, Cooley and his band played popular swing-shift dances, staging late-night shows for those who got off work after midnight. His broad-based popularity and the expertise of his band led to his first #1 hit, "Shame on You," in 1945.

Meanwhile, perceptive songwriters such as Cindy Walker also succeeded in California's vibrant country community. Walker provided a bounty of songs for Wills, including "Cherokee Maiden" and "Bubbles in My Beer," as well as writing songs for westerns (Gene Autry's hit "Blue Canadian Rockies") and other Hollywood films. Walker's career extended for decades, encompassing such classics as Ernest Tubb's "Warm Red Wine," Eddy Arnold's "You Don't Know Me" (also a hit for Ray Charles), and Roy Orbison's "Dream Baby (How Long Must I Dream)."

During the 1950s and 1960s, Los Angeles and Bakersfield joined Nashville as country music centers with Buck Owens, Merle Haggard, Glen Campbell, and Dwight Yoakam among those who continued that legacy. Their success proved that country music's popularity knew no geographic boundaries.

Hank Thompson

Spade Cooley

Above: Hank Thompson's leather stage jacket made by Nudie the Rodeo Tailor.

Left: Spade Cooley's fiddle.

28

SETTIN' THE WOODS ON FIRE:

NEW SOUNDS ON THE JUKEBOX

As country music expanded from coast to coast, the southern regions where it first came to life continued to develop new ways to energize the genre to fit the times. In the 1940s, two new sounds surfaced, one born of urban nightspots and rural roadhouses, the other bringing instrumental fire and vocal splendor to traditional string music.

As performers began appearing in rough-and-tumble clubs, they created by necessity a louder, amplified musical style driven by keening fiddles, electric guitars, and steel guitars; it became known as honky-tonk. Meanwhile, a willful Kentucky mandolinist, Bill Monroe, forged a dynamic stringband sound emphasizing the banjo, fiddle, and

Ira Louvin's 1922 Gibson F-4 mandolin.

Lester Flatt and Earl Scruggs

Ira and Charlie Louvin

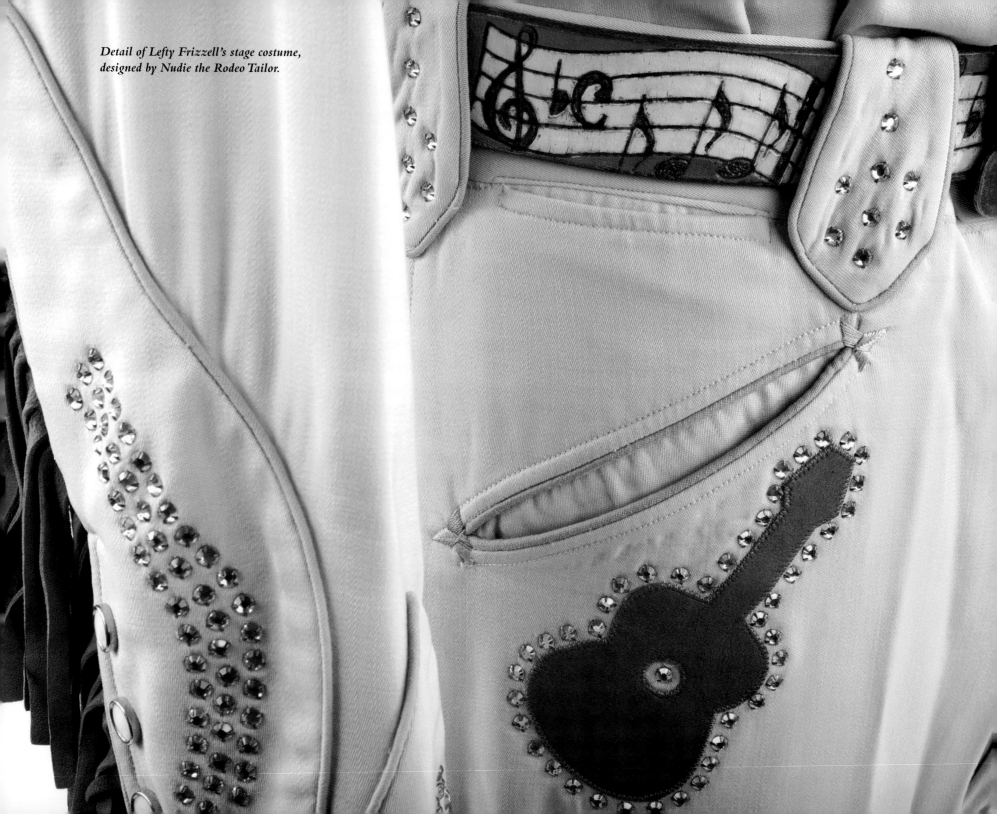

Detail of Lefty Frizzell's stage costume, designed by Nudie the Rodeo Tailor.

harmony vocals as well as his own virtuoso mandolin work. This new genre would be named bluegrass, after Monroe's band, the Blue Grass Boys.

Honky-tonk appealed to young people who left their "home out on the rural route," as Hank Williams sang, and to hard-working folks who wanted to blow off steam. Played on electrified instruments with enough volume to be heard over a rowdy crowd, honky-tonk songs dealt with loss, spiritual desolation, and the difficulties of relationships in a time of change. These songs also celebrated stepping out on Saturday night and the temptations of the evening.

Bluegrass emerged during this same period, a rhythmically driven style rooted in the conservative morals of family and religion. Tightly arranged and played with propulsive precision, the music challenged instrumentalists to reach new heights. Monroe and banjoist Earl Scruggs pushed the music forward with virtuosity and vision, creating an aesthetically adventurous sound still grounded in tradition.

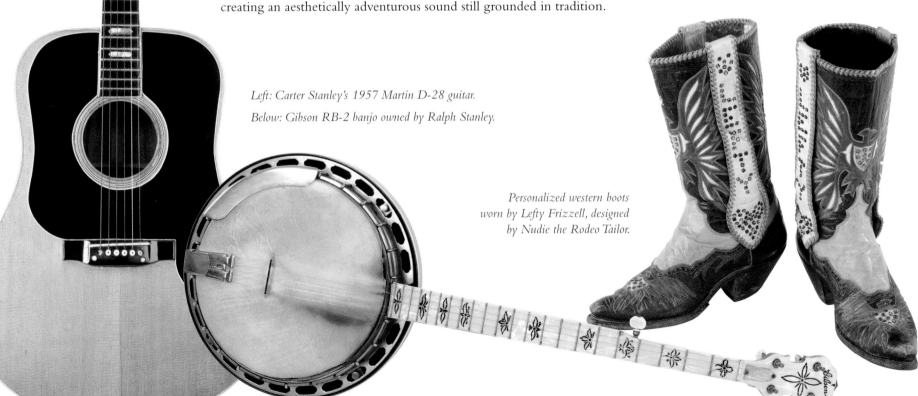

Left: Carter Stanley's 1957 Martin D-28 guitar.
Below: Gibson RB-2 banjo owned by Ralph Stanley.

Personalized western boots worn by Lefty Frizzell, designed by Nudie the Rodeo Tailor.

Hank Snow

Carter and Ralph Stanley

Lefty Frizzell

The music created by Monroe and Flatt & Scruggs inspired generations of vocalists and musicians. Both the Stanley Brothers and the Louvin Brothers explored the power of sky-high harmonies and stripped-down acousti arrangements, with the former emerging as bluegrass stalwarts and the latter growing into an influential country and gospel act.

Honky-tonk would prove similarly flexible. Practitioners such as Hank Snow opened it up to include blues, Hawaiian music, and Latin influences, while stylists like Lefty Frizzell proved the music could include sentimentality and humor, with Frizzell's note-bending vocals exerting a strong influence on stalwarts such as George Jones, Merle Haggard, John Anderson, Randy Travis, Keith Whitley, and Alan Jackson.

Hank Snow's stage costume, created by Nudie the Rodeo Tailor, based on Snow's hit song "Golden Rocket."

Elvis Presley

The Everly Brothers at RCA Studio B

LET'S HAVE A PARTY:

REAL GONE COUNTRY

When rock & roll stomped, swiveled, and shook its way onto the American cultural scene, it rattled the entire music industry. The music's youth appeal cut into country music's popularity and sales, and it influenced Nashville's future in several ways.

But country music played a direct role in rock & roll's birth. Nearly all of the groundbreaking songs created at Sun Studios in Memphis—an early epicenter of rock & roll—drew on country traditions and Beale Street blues.

Elvis Presley made that connection explicit with his first single, a cover of Mississippi-based bluesman Arthur Crudup's "That's All Right" as the A-side, and a speeded-up version of bluegrass pioneer Bill Monroe's "Blue Moon of Kentucky" as its B-side. The coupling illustrated how this brash new sound married blues and country traditions, energized by youthful abandon.

Carl Perkins's blue suede shoes.

Carl Perkins and his band.

All of Sun's legendary rock & rollers came from poor, rural, southern backgrounds, and they grew up worshipping the Grand Ole Opry. Yet Jerry Lee Lewis, Carl Perkins, Johnny Cash, and Charlie Rich likely wouldn't have received a recording contract in Nashville—even though all of them were sooner or later embraced by country fans. It took a record label willing to gamble on an impetuous new sound for rock & roll to grow into a national phenomenon.

Of course, some country musicians drew inspiration from rock & roll, too, as heard in Marty Robbins's "Don't Worry" and Sonny James's "Young Love." As country singer Bob Luman said, after hearing Elvis Presley in concert, "That's the last time I tried to sing like Webb Pierce or Lefty Frizzell."

Left: Stage costume shirt worn by Jerry Lee Lewis.

Right: Leather jackets worn by Don Everly (right) and Phil Everly (left).

Jerry Lee Lewis   *Brenda Lee*   *Wanda Jackson*

Indeed, a generation of rockabilly artists heated up the airwaves with a wild blend of hillbilly music and rock & roll attitude. One of the best-known rockabilly songs of the 1950s, "Blue Suede Shoes," came from Carl Perkins, a former field worker from Tiptonville, Tennessee, who cited the Opry and music he heard from black sharecroppers as the primary sources of his sound.

Nashville also recorded rock & roll hits, with the Everly Brothers (produced by Chet Atkins), Brenda Lee (produced by Owen Bradley), and Roy Orbison (produced by Fred Foster) among the best-known stars in Nashville's rock countdown. Elvis, after leaving Sun Records for RCA, recorded many classic hits at RCA Studio B, in the heart of Nashville's Music Row neighborhood.

Wanda Jackson's 1959 Martin D-28 guitar and fringed stage costume.

Patsy Cline

SWEET DREAMS:
THE NASHVILLE SOUND

Nashville responded to rock & roll by evolving toward a more cosmopolitan sound. In Music Row studios, fiddles and steel guitars gave way to lush orchestrations and honeyed harmonies. Producers Chet Atkins and Owen Bradley relied on skilled studio musicians—the "A Team"—whose creative input and quick adaptability made them vital to the hit-making process.

The appealing style they created became known as the Nashville Sound. It included vocalists Patsy Cline and Jim Reeves, whose rich tones and clear enunciation worked well with sophisticated arrangements. Imaginative singer-songwriters like Don Gibson benefited from modern sounds that focused attention on their inventive wordplay.

Jim Reeves

Cocktail gown worn by Patsy Cline.

Cufflinks, button covers, and red patent leather shoes worn by Jim Reeves.

A few Nashville veterans adapted well to the polished production style. Eddy Arnold, Ray Price, and Marty Robbins found that their voices blended well with urbane flourishes. Similarly, female singers Skeeter Davis and Dottie West created enduring recordings that brought new listeners to country music.

Meanwhile, the newly formed Country Music Association marshaled the industry's forces to more actively promote its songs and stars to radio stations, the media, and advertisers. Suddenly, the popular appeal of country music became more visible, leading to more growth.

Some country traditionalists balked at such moves, complaining that the uptown sounds took country music too far from its down-home roots. But Nashville continued to present artists with traditional styles alongside the sweetened productions of some of its stars.

Country music has always been a big-tent genre that responds to changes in popular culture by bringing in new influences. The Nashville Sound was a reaction to its times—as well another step in the genre's ongoing evolution.

Marty Robbins

Don Gibson

Above: Stage costume jacket made for Don Gibson by Nudie the Rodeo Tailor.

Left: Small 1957 Martin 5-18 guitar, played by Marty Robbins.

Ray Price

Charley Pride

SWINGING DOORS:
THE RETURN OF HARD COUNTRY

Not everyone in the country music insdustry believed that rock & roll drowned out the appeal of straight-up country music. Indeed, many performers seized the moment to enliven old-school, fiddle-and-steel sounds with inventive rhythms, piercing harmonies, and memorable songwriting.

Ray Price, for one, juiced Texas honky-tonk with a catchy shuffle beat and western swing-style soloing. He employed a four-four rhythm reinforced by drums and special walking bass lines, providing a dance-floor foundation for jazzy fiddle and steel runs and Price's soaring voice. With two-stepping specialties like "Crazy Arms" and "City Lights," Price combined honky-tonk and swing into a fresh, energized sound that inspired generations of artists and fans.

Meanwhile, the oil-and-agriculture town of Bakersfield, California, became home to a stripped-down country sound that captured the attention of many transplanted Americans chased west by Depression Era dust storms.

Buck Owens and his band, the Buckaroos, fashioned a hot country sound that took rock's energy and filtered it through

Right: Ray Price's stage jacket,
created by Nudie the Rodeo Tailor.

Personalized label sewn into the lining of Ray Price's stage jacket.

40

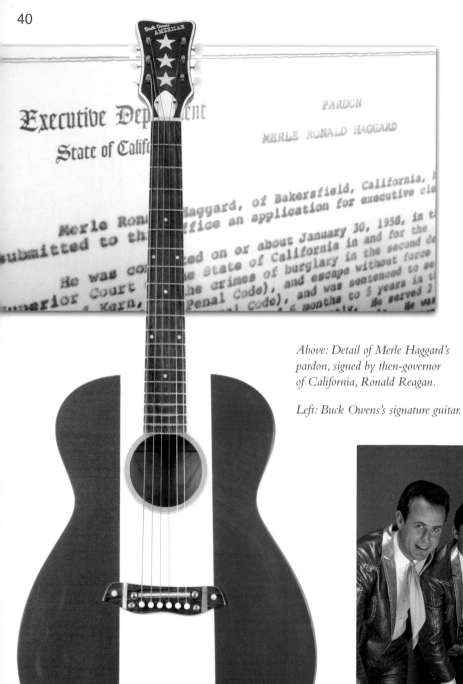

Executive Department

State of Calif...

PARDON

MERLE RONALD HAGGARD

Merle Ron...aggard, of Bakersfield, California,...
submitted to th...fice an application for executive cle...

He was co...ed on or about January 30, 1958, in t...
...rior Court...he State of California in and for the...
...Kern,...he crimes of burglary in the second de...
...Penal Code), and escape without force...
...enal Code),...and was sentenced to se...
...months to 5 years in t...
...He served 2...

Above: Detail of Merle Haggard's pardon, signed by then-governor of California, Ronald Reagan.

Left: Buck Owens's signature guitar.

a country sensibility packed with loads of personality and talent. By the mid-1960s, Owens hits such as "Tiger by the Tail" and "Act Naturally" firmly established his music as a counterpoint to the smooth Nashville Sound.

Bakersfield soon produced another Country Music Hall of Fame member when Merle Haggard swaggered forth with fiercely concise barroom music buoyed by heartfelt songs torn from his wayward youth, his personal struggles, and his views on American society.

Nashville served up its share of tradition-leaning country stars as well. Faron Young packed a punch with honky-tonk songs that filled a vacuum left by the death of his hero, Hank Williams. The raucous 1955 hit "Live Fast, Love Hard, Die Young," Young's first #1, proved that Music City still produced songs with rough edges.

Buck Owens & the Buckaroos

Merle Haggard

Faron Young

Connie Smith

Connie Smith, a reserved young family woman from Ohio, hit #1 with her first release, "Once a Day," establishing herself as one of the great traditional singers of her era. Arriving in Nashville amid the Civil Rights Era, Charley Pride established his traditional country bona fides with a deep, down-home voice that made him one of the most popular old-school singers of his generation. Both Smith and Pride would endure for decades, proudly carrying their traditional country sounds into the twenty-first century, to the delight of country fans worldwide.

Left: Connie Smith's 1963 Gibson Dove guitar.

Right: Gay guitar personalized for Faron Young.

Upper Right: Faron Young's fringed suede jacket.

41

COUNTRY COUTURE

*Detail from stage costume
designed for Hank Snow.*

NUDIE THE RODEO TAILOR

Nudie Cohn brought flash and sparkle to western-wear costumes, a look that became synonymous with country music from the 1940s through the 1960s. Setting up shop in Hollywood as Nudie the Rodeo Tailor, Cohn created custom-designed stage wear for everyone from Gene Autry and Hank Williams to Elvis Presley and Gram Parsons.

Below: Stage costume created for Merle Haggard, early 1970s.

Clothing label for Nudie's Rodeo Tailors.

Cover of catalog for Nudie's Rodeo Tailors.

Left: Boots created for Hank Thompson, based on his song "Humpty Dumpty Heart."

Above: Stage costume designed for Lefty Frizzell.

NATHAN TURK

From the 1930s to the 1970s, western-wear designer Nathan Turk created lavishly embroidered stage costumes for country singers and celluloid cowboys. His clients included the Maddox Brothers & Rose, who earned billing as "the most colorful hillbilly band in the land." Other regular customers included Roy Rogers, Hank Snow, Hank Thompson, and Ernest Tubb.

Above: Nathan Turk clothing label.

Far left: Stage costume worn by Fred Maddox.

Left: Stage costume designed for Buck Owens and worn onstage at his 1966 Carnegie Hall concert.

Right: Stagewear designed for Rose Maddox.

*Detail of stage costume
worn by Don Maddox.*

DREAMING MY DREAMS:
THE JOURNEY CONTINUES

By the 1960s, country music was an established American art form. Mirroring American life, the music of the ensuing decades included experimentation, fragmentation, resolve, a longing for tradition, and a race to keep up with technological advances.

As with society at large, the world of country music experienced highs and lows. But the right songs always surfaced to keep country music relevant and entertaining. The music communicated what changed about America—and what stayed the same. Country songs continued to address the trials, the triumphs, and the yearning for freedom, for love, for family, for community, and for the right to pursue the American dream.

Brad Paisley's first electric guitar, a Sears Silvertone, with amplifier and speaker built into the guitar case.

dreaming
MY DREAMS
THE JOURNEY CONTINUES
1960s to the Present

Roger Miller

Johnny Cash

WHEN TWO WORLDS COLLIDE:
COUNTRY MEETS MASS MARKET

By the mid-1960s, a new crop of talent made it clear country music would continue to flourish despite the rise of rock & roll. Thanks to several distinctly gifted performers, country made inroads into the mainstream of American culture in ways it hadn't in previous decades.

Roger Miller brought an air of hipster élan to his iconoclastic music. Songs such as "King of the Road" and "Dang Me" were unlike anything before them, using unusual yet infectious arrangements that matched Miller's clever wordplay and his skewed perspective on society. Johnny Cash, marching to his own beat, delved into folk songs, protest music, and controversial topics, along the way appealing to everyone from Folsom Prison inmates to young rockers to U.S. presidents.

Eleven Grammy awards won by Roger Miller in 1964 and 1965.

ITS KNOWING THAT YOUR DOOR IS ALWAYS OPEN
& YOUR PATH IS FREE TO WALK
THAT MAKES ME TEND TO LEAVE MY SLEEPING BAG
ROLLED UP & STASHED BEHIND YOUR COUCH
IT'S KNOWING I'M NOT SHACKLED BY FORGOTTEN WORDS
AND BONDS, OR THE INK STAINS THAT HAVE
DRIED UP ON SOME LINE
THAT KEEPS YOU ON THE BACK ROADS BY THE RIVERS
OF MY MEMORIES, AND KEEPS YOU EVER
GENTLE ON MY MIND

ITS NOT CLINGING TO THE ROCKS & IVY PLANTED
ON SOME COLUMN NOW THAT BINDS ME
BECAUSE THE
OR SOMETHING THAT SOMEBODY SAID, ~~BROKEN~~

Johnny Cash's 1968 Martin D-35 guitar.

Cash's success lured counterculture singer-songwriters such as Kris Kristofferson to Nashville. A Rhodes Scholar and former Army captain who piloted fighter jets, Kristofferson brought a new frankness and sensitivity to Nashville songwriting. Cash recorded "Sunday Morning Coming Down," a poetic portrayal of a down-and-outer dealing with loneliness, while Kristofferson's "Help Me Make It Through the Night" and "For the Good Times" addressed romantic relationships and sexuality in candidly intimate terms.

Like Kristofferson, Tom T. Hall developed an individual style that crossed literary storytelling with lyrics dealing with those living on the edges of society. Steeped in bluegrass during his youth in Kentucky, Hall broke songwriting conventions in such hits as "A Week in a Country Jail" and "(Old Dogs, Children and) Watermelon Wine."

Dolly Parton, like Hall, emerged from Appalachia to have a great impact on country music. She first gained notice as the duet partner of successful country singer and TV host Porter Wagoner, then as a singer-songwriter who captured the impoverished mountain life in hits such as "Coat of Many Colors." Eventually, she became

Tom T. Hall's briefcase, with his manuscript for "Loretta Lynn Waltz."

Tom T. Hall

Glen Campbell

a world-renowned crossover artist with her classics "I Will Always Love You" and "9 to 5," as well as a successful actress, entrepreneur, and philanthropist.

Arkansas native Glen Campbell became a star thanks to hosting a popular network TV show, *The Glen Campbell Goodtime Hour*, while issuing a series of imaginative story songs, including "Wichita Lineman" and "Galveston," that showcased his capable tenor voice and guitar work.

In an era of great social upheaval, country music continued to evolve with the times. Its songs reflected changes going on in the culture while maintaining the earthy, honest quality that gave the music its identity.

Right: John Hartford's Baldwin banjo.

Below: Dolly Parton's manuscript for "Jolene."

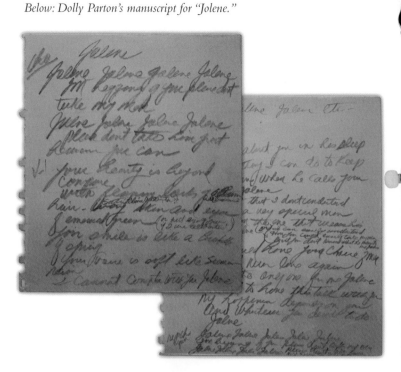

Dolly Parton

Kris Kristofferson

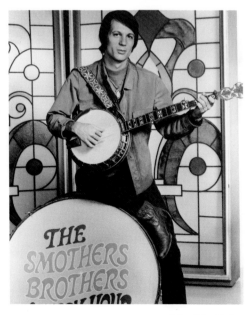

John Hartford

Ray Charles and Johnny Cash

NASHVILLE SKYLINE:

ROCKING BACK TO THE COUNTRY

In another sign of country music's growing popularity, many big names from other fields—including Ray Charles, the Byrds, and Bob Dylan—drew heavily on country influences in the 1960s.

Ray Charles's 1962 album *Modern Sounds in Country and Western Music* re-imagined classic country songs as lush, soulful ballads and brassy uptempo numbers. His take on Don Gibson's soaring ballad "I Can't Stop Loving You" spent five weeks at #1 on the *Billboard* pop charts.

Bob Dylan first employed Nashville musicians in 1966 for his landmark album *Blonde on Blonde*; another Nashville album, *John Wesley Harding*, followed in 1967. Citing Hank Williams and Johnny Cash as major influences, Dylan more fully revealed his country side on 1969's *Nashville Skyline*. That year, Dylan also made a rare network TV appearance on *The Johnny Cash Show*, performing three songs, including a duet with Cash on Dylan's "Girl from the North Country."

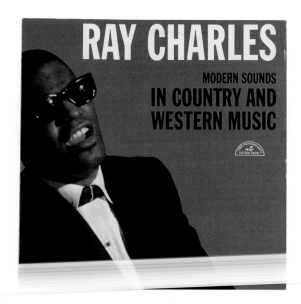

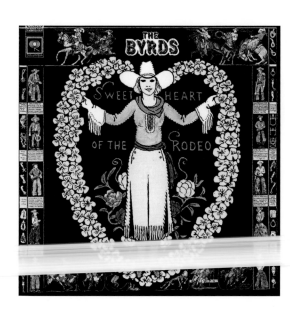

The Flying Burrito Brothers

Emmylou Harris

Left: Stage costume worn by Gram Parsons and created for him by Nudie the Rodeo Tailor.

Below: Emmylou Harris's 1955 Gibson J-200 guitar with rose inlay.

Nitty Gritty Dirt Band

Customized washboard played by Jeff Hanna, and 1970 Martin D-41 played by Jim Ibbotson, both members of the Nitty Gritty Dirt Band.

The Byrds already were a successful folk-rock act, with former bluegrass player Chris Hillman in the band, when Gram Parsons joined, resulting in the band's 1968 country-rock masterpiece, *Sweetheart of the Rodeo*. Recorded in Nashville, and featuring contributions by country musicians Lloyd Green and John Hartford, the album included songs by Merle Haggard, the Louvin Brothers, and Cindy Walker as well as originals by Parsons.

In 1971, a folk-rock group based in Southern California created a sprawling, well-received project that united legendary country and folk musicians with shaggy-haired acolytes. The Nitty Gritty Dirt Band brought together historic figures Roy Acuff, Maybelle Carter, Earl Scruggs, Merle Travis, Doc Watson, and others for a three-LP collection of classic covers and original songs.

Many other long-haired rock musicians began incorporating country music into their sounds. As the 1970s progressed, successful country-influenced performers such as the Eagles, Emmylou Harris, and Linda Ronstadt garnered many hits, and country-rock grew into a staple of rock and pop radio.

56

LONG HAIRED COUNTRY BOYS:
SOUTHERN ROCK GOES COUNTRY

By the close of the 1970s, the boundary between country and rock bands had blurred even more. After the Allman Brothers introduced a new form of southern rock—with a multiracial lineup that drew on blues, country, folk, jazz, and rock—other young musicians began blending similar influences. Displaying youthful energy and a renewed southern pride, these bands helped the South move beyond the Civil Rights Era toward a period of musical and social integration.

Charlie Daniels and Hank Williams Jr. began scoring hits on the country charts while touting their links to the Marshall Tucker Band and Lynyrd Skynyrd, two southern bands heard on rock radio. A fiddler, guitarist, and songwriter from North

Left: Boots owned by Hank Williams Jr., customized with his phoenix logo.
Right: Gibson Les Paul electric guitar played by Charlie Daniels.

Hank Williams Jr.

Charlie Daniels

Carolina, Daniels first logged rock hits with "Long Haired Country Boy" and "The South's Gonna Do It" before taking "The Devil Went Down to Georgia" to #1 on the country charts. Daniels continued to record hits, such as "Drinkin' My Baby Goodbye," through the 1980s.

Hank Williams Jr. started out performing his father's songs, but established his own identity by recording with southern rock musicians. After a near-fatal fall on a Montana mountain, Williams reinvented himself with the country-rock hits "Family Tradition" and "A Country Boy Can Survive." He went on to become the CMA Entertainer of the Year in 1987 and 1988 and the ACM Entertainer of the Year from 1986 to 1988.

By the beginning of the 1980s, a band named for its founders' home state—Alabama—put a polished spin on southern rock. With an extended string of #1 hits and million-selling albums, cousins Randy Owen, Teddy Gentry, and Jeff Cook, along with drummer Mark Herndon, showed how country themes and rock dynamics could be woven into a sound that captivated country audiences.

After Alabama's success, rock became a primary influence on country artists as generations of musicians grew up listening to both musical forms.

Alabama

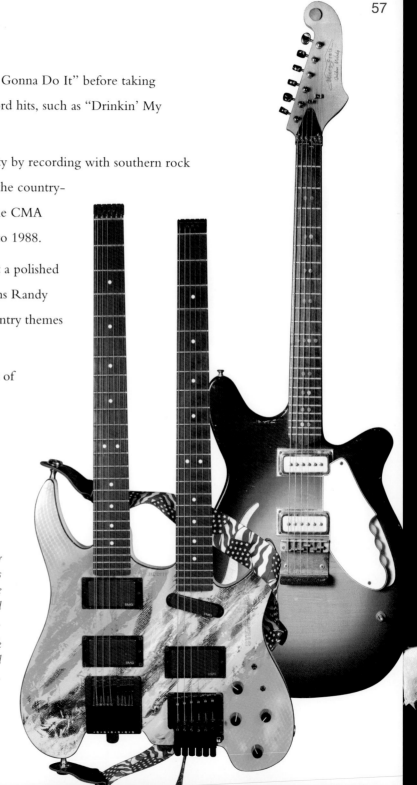

Far right: Electric guitar played by Alabama's Randy Owen in the 1970s, when the band was called Wildcountry.

Right: Double-neck Steinberger guitar played by Alabama's Jeff Cook.

Tammy Wynette

George Jones

YOU'RE LOOKING AT COUNTRY:
THE OLD WAYS PREVAIL

Southern rock and the outlaw sounds of Willie Nelson and Waylon Jennings represented country music's tendency to reinvent itself to reflect societal changes. At the same time, several performers held tightly to country's traditional styles.

George Jones, Loretta Lynn, and Tammy Wynette embodied country's fundamental values. Through the 1960s and 1970s, these country stars proudly sang about hard times and bedrock principles. From dirt-poor rural backgrounds, these artists maintained country-proud personas that drew the devotion of fans.

Whether singing honky-tonk or lushly produced ballads, Jones always sounded stone-cold country, with his note-slurring style and his heart-tugging themes. His classic song "He Stopped Loving Her Today" may soar with orchestrations and harmonies, but it's country to the core.

Above right: Beaded gown worn by Tammy Wynette.
Below right: Suit worn by George Jones.

Tanya Tucker

Johnny Paycheck

Loretta Lynn

Similarly, Johnny Paycheck delivered audacious lyrics with an emotionally vibrant technique comparable to Jones. Loretta Lynn drew attention with her autobiographical songs, which were as down-home as the Kentucky twang in her instantly identifiable voice. Lynn addressed topics important to women of her time—marriage, family, self-identity, the rise of female empowerment—with spirited words that working-class wives could understand.

Tammy Wynette, with her distinct vocal style, sounded fragile yet resilient while addressing the roles of women. Jones, Lynn, and Wynette all influenced younger singers such as Tanya Tucker, a spitfire youngster with a big voice and a bold stage presence.

As usual, no matter how far country expanded its sound with new influences, a handful of hard-core traditionalists remained anchored by the genre's sturdiest roots.

Above right: : Loretta Lynn's Gibson J-50 guitar with custom pickguard.

Below Right: Johnny Paycheck's Custom Tobias electric guitar.

A select few musical instruments have become country music icons. The music fashioned on them helped shape American culture.

CHET ATKINS'S D'ANGELICO EXCEL

The guitars John D'Angelico of Brooklyn, New York, built by hand from 1932 to 1964 are considered works of art and are highly prized by both players and collectors. To Chet Atkins, acquiring one of the stylish D'Angelicos was the equivalent of getting a Rolls-Royce. Not long after he purchased it, in 1950, Atkins modified the instrument, adding a metal bridge, a Vibrola bar, two pickups, volume controls, a cord jack, and a pickup selector switch.

During the early 1950s, while establishing himself as a session guitarist and a solo artist, Atkins used the guitar almost exclusively. He also played it on his appearances as a sideman with Mother Maybelle and the Carter Sisters. During a radio show in 1953, June Carter accidentally knocked the guitar off its stand and broke the neck. The D'Angelico was later restored, and Atkins recorded with it again on his 1996 album, *Almost Alone*.

These treasures are currently displayed as part of the museum's collection—and serve as enduring symbols of the power of music.

HANK WILLIAMS'S MARTIN D-28

Hank Williams used this 1944 Martin D-28 guitar to create his unsurpassed legacy as a country singer and songwriter. Among the instruments he owned, this is regarded as his finest. The scratches on its top reflect the wear and tear of countless personal appearances made by the charismatic Williams, everywhere from nightclubs and outdoor concerts to national television.

After Williams's tragic death at age twenty-nine, on New Year's Eve, 1952, the guitar passed into the possession of his family. It was handed down to Hank Williams Jr., who kept alive the family tradition by using it occasionally in performance. Hank Jr. preserved the guitar for the most part as his father had left it, with its original herringbone edge trim, ebony fretboard with slotted diamond inlays, and wartime-style tuners with plastic, white oval buttons.

Dottie West

Kenny Rogers

POP GOES THE COUNTRY:
CROSSOVER FEVER SPREADS

After pop singers Olivia Newton-John and John Denver received Country Music Association awards in the mid-1970s, some Nashville insiders protested. They feared that the infiltration of pop acts on the country music charts could dilute the genre's identity and make the music too homogenized.

At the same time, some country music stars and several newcomers to the genre presented a middle-of-the-road sound that blended country and pop influences. Perhaps drawn by the increased sales that came from crossover success, or perhaps simply following their own muses and drawing on their own influences, these pop-country acts found an enthusiastic audience, and their broad appeal strongly affected the direction of country music.

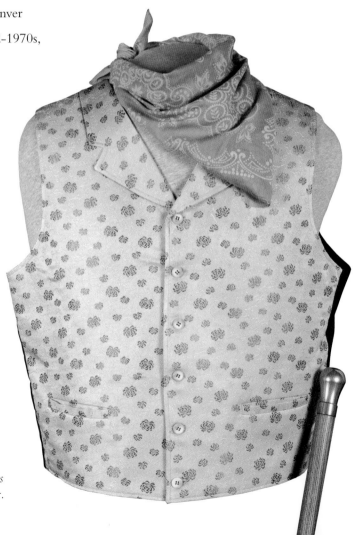

Vest, bandanna, and walking stick used by Kenny Rogers while filming the 1980 movie The Gambler.

Detail from Dottie West's stage costume.

Some of those enjoying the greatest crossover success had backgrounds in other genres. Kenny Rogers had recorded pop hits as leader of the First Edition, although he regularly had drawn on Nashville songwriters for material. Acclaimed country songwriter Mickey Newbury wrote the First Edition hit "Just Dropped In (to See What Condition My Condition Was In)," and country star Mel Tillis wrote another of the band's hits, "Ruby, Don't Take Your Love to Town." As a solo act, Rogers took aim at the country charts and scored massive hits with "The Gambler" and "Lucille," as well as recording many hit duets, including "Islands in the Stream" with Dolly Parton.

Ronnie Milsap recorded soul music in Memphis before finding greater success in Nashville with dramatic, pop-leaning fare, such as "Daydreams About Night Things" and "It Was Almost Like a Song." Like Rogers, Milsap's country shift resulted in numerous top hits and made him a popular concert act. Don Williams also

Ronnie Milsap *Don Williams*

Don Williams's 1978 Ovation Legend guitar.

had early pop hits as a member of a vocal group, the Pozo-Seco Singers. His laid-back persona and relaxed Texas baritone made him a natural for country stardom, and his many hits include "Tulsa Time" and "Good Ole Boys Like Me."

Meanwhile, many singers who began with more traditional sounds—such as Mel Tillis and Dottie West—drew new audiences when adding pop polish to their recordings. Tillis's comic persona also got him work as an actor. As both a soloist and in duets with Kenny Rogers, West donned glittering show-business outfits and sold out venues in Las Vegas.

After these success stories, other artists gravitated toward pop-country sounds, and crossover material found a home on country radio that has continued through the decades.

Mel Tillis

Ronnie Milsap's dark glasses.

Above right: Embroidered jacket created for Mel Tillis by Manuel.
Lower right: Mel Tillis's CMA award for Entertainer of the Year, 1976.

Ricky Skaggs

Reba McEntire

TELL ME 'BOUT THE GOOD OLD DAYS:
COUNTRY LOOKS HOMEWARD

The 1980 blockbuster film *Urban Cowboy* spotlighted a country dance scene flourishing in spacious nightclubs such as Gilley's in Pasadena, Texas. When the movie became a hit, it inspired a rush on sales of western-style clothing and country albums, some of it leaning toward kitsch. As a result, the term "urban cowboy" came to stand for a watered-down version of the country lifestyle.

As the fad ended, a new generation of country artists arrived to re-energize Music Row. Drawing inspiration from the down-to-earth sounds of country music's past, these "new traditionalists," as the media called them, proved that straight-ahead country music could be refashioned to appeal to young music fans.

Several of the new stars came from familiar outposts: Ricky Skaggs and the Judds had roots in the Kentucky mountains, George Strait rode in from the plains of Texas, and Reba McEntire brought her big voice from the prairies of Oklahoma. Each developed a distinctly individual style that would influence the course of country music—and provide each with careers that spanned decades.

Ricky Skaggs's Gibson A-40 mandolin.

Bill Monroe and Ricky Skaggs

George Strait

The Judds

Ricky Skaggs spent years under the tutelage of bluegrass greats before joining Emmylou Harris's renowned Hot Band. From there, he launched a solo career with an exciting hybrid of bluegrass and contemporary country music that resulted in a string of top hits and awards.

Similarly, the Judds used stripped-down, acoustic-based music highlighting Wynonna Judd's husky voice and the sweet harmonies of her mother, Naomi Judd. Combining grassroots and glamour, they became arena headliners until a chronic illness forced Naomi Judd from the road. Wynonna continued as a hit solo artist, while Naomi recovered and became a successful author and television star.

George Strait almost singlehandedly revived cowboy fashion and western-swing influences in country music; his movie-star looks, humble stage manner, and steadfast dedication to older

Stage costume worn by George Strait.

musical styles led him to become one of the biggest stars of his era. His enduring success resulted in a record-breaking accumulation of #1 hits, and he continued to sell out concerts nationwide several decades into his career.

Reba McEntire showed similar resiliency, but the one-time traditionalist gained her enduring stardom by constantly updating her image and music. Her personality and ambition took her to starring roles in films, on Broadway, and in her own TV sitcom.

Country music would swing back toward pop and rock influences, but the 1980s proved that Nashville could rebound from a drop in popularity and reset its future with a fresh crop of artists who honor the music's roots.

Left: Reba McEntire's boots, styled after a pair owned by Patsy Cline.

Right: The Judds' CMA awards for Vocal Group of the Year in 1986, and Single of the Year, in 1985; and ACM awards for Top Vocal Duet, 1989, and Vocal Duet of the Year, 1990.

Far right: Wynonna Judd's Gibson Les Paul "WY-2K" guitar, used during the Judds' 2000 Reunion Tour.

Rosanne Cash

Rodney Crowell

GUITARS, CADILLACS:
COUNTRY MUSIC'S NEW WAVE

The success of Reba McEntire, George Strait, and other new traditionalists proved country music fans would welcome young performers. Consequently, Nashville's gates opened to new artists who revolutionized country music's look and sound.

The youth movement was symbolized by a deep-voiced traditionalist, Randy Travis, whose debut album, *Storms of Life*, sold three million copies—a rare feat for a country newcomer at the time.

Rosanne Cash and Rodney Crowell, who were married from 1979 to 1992 and often collaborated on each other's solo recordings, presented a smart, crisp take on country and roots-rock that addressed the lives of young adults in modern ways.

Top right: Manuscript for "I Hardly Know How to Be Myself," co-written by Rodney Crowell and Rosanne Cash.

Lower right: Stetson bowler hat and custom western boots worn by Rosanne Cash.

Randy Travis   *Dwight Yoakam*   *Steve Earle*

Steve Earle swaggered forward with terse, guitar-driven roots-rock that tackled working-class issues and addressed personal demons. Lyle Lovett, a Texas songwriter like Crowell and Earle, drew on swing and folk-blues to explore family, alienation, and modern relationships in idiosyncratic, literary terms.

Dwight Yoakam, a Kentucky-born performer and actor based in Los Angeles, brought a Bakersfield-influenced brashness to his Telecaster-fired country rock.

Together, these and other 1980s artists broadened country music's appeal to fans weaned on the singer-songwriters and folk-rockers of the 1970s, helping set the stage for even greater growth in country music in the 1990s.

Right: Fringed suede jacket worn by Randy Travis.

Far right: Stage costume worn by Dwight Yoakam, including jacket designed by Manuel.

WEBB PIERCE'S 1962 PONTIAC BONNEVILLE

Some entertainers enjoyed custom-designed cars as flashy as their stage wear.

Webb Pierce's 1962 Pontiac Bonneville features ornamental pistols and rifles on the hood and handles, horseshoes for pedals, and more than a thousand silver dollars in the tooled-leather upholstery. A mock saddle serves as the console between the front bucket seats.

Hollywood fashion king Nudie the Rodeo Tailor, a favorite of country stars, custom-designed the Pontiac. Six were built, each with a selling price of $20,000.

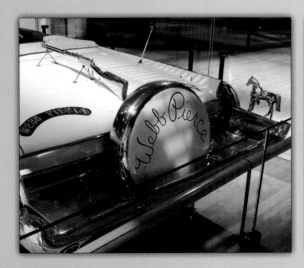

ELVIS PRESLEY'S 1960 CADILLAC LIMOUSINE

Elvis Presley's 1960 Cadillac limousine includes gold-plated highlights and forty coats of paint containing crushed diamonds and fish scales.

The luxurious back seat features a small television console with an antenna for reception, a state-of-the-art stereo system complete with a record player operated by the rear passengers, an early version of a car phone, and a communication system so those in back could talk with the driver.

The car was created specifically for Presley by Barris Kustom City of North Hollywood, with Presley personally involved in its design.

Martina McBride

Vince Gill

POCKET FULL OF GOLD:

COUNTRY IN THE AGE OF PLENTY

In September 1991, Garth Brooks became the first country music artist to have an album debut at the top spot on *Billboard* magazine's chart of best-selling albums in the nation, spanning all genres. The feat coincided with the arrival of a new technology that tallied sales totals at the cash register rather than by reports from retailers. Removing bias from the procedure, it became apparent that country albums were selling in greater numbers than previously reported—and that Garth Brooks was the hottest recording artist in America.

Brooks's enormous sales power, and that of veterans such as George Strait and newcomers such as Alan Jackson and Vince Gill, astonished the media and the music industry. Simultaneously, country radio ruled the airwaves. Country music officially had entered the American entertainment mainstream.

Buoyed by this success, Nashville flooded the market with attractive young men in cowboy hats and western attire—inspiring the term "hat act." The best of these singers distinguished themselves, usually by combining traditional and contemporary sounds in distinctive

Garth Brooks's 1969 Martin D-28 acoustic guitar.

Patty Loveless

Faith Hill

Tim McGraw

ways. Several women, including Patty Loveless, Martina McBride, and LeAnn Rimes, also mixed the old with the new in an engaging manner.

Brooks cited "my two Georges"—Jones and Strait—as his influences, but also acknowledged a debt to singer-songwriters James Taylor and Dan Fogelberg and arena-rock acts KISS and Kansas. The results balanced acoustic balladry with barroom country music and classic rock, all of which Brooks helped sell with a dynamic stage show.

Alan Jackson took a more laid-back approach, mixing autobiographical songs with hard-core honky-tonk. In performance, he performed his hits in a humble yet engaging manner, as did his heroes Jones, Strait, and Don Williams.

Far left: Stage costume worn by Patty Loveless.

Left: Leather jacket worn by Tim McGraw in his video for "Indian Outlaw."

Vince Gill blended his background in bluegrass and country music into a sensitive yet stirring style that highlighted his beautiful tenor voice and his dazzling musicality on guitar.

Other early '90s successes included Tim McGraw, who caught fire with clever sing-alongs and touching ballads, but soon expanded his sound with rock influences that brought greater sophistication to his messages. His wife, Faith Hill, followed a similar path, beginning with lighthearted up-tempo tunes and love ballads, but evolving into works that pushed country's boundaries in sound and theme.

By the new century, country artists regularly topped the *Billboard* all-genre charts and frequently appeared on television and in films—maintaining the strides made during country's 1990s explosion.

Alan Jackson

LeAnn Rimes

Above: Alan Jackson's leather suit jacket.

Left: Vince Gill's first guitar.

Sam Bush

Del McCoury

OUR ROOTS ARE SHOWING:
COUNTRY ALTERNATIVES

At the end of the twentieth century, organized support increased for artists drawing on country's musical traditions but working outside its commercial mainstream. Two industry trade groups, the Americana Music Association and the International Bluegrass Music Association, supported a growing membership with marketing efforts, annual conventions, and awards programs honoring significant performers of the past and present.

Released in 2000, the film *O Brother, Where Art Thou?* generated a Grammy-winning soundtrack and subsequent concert tours, lifting the profile of the Americana and bluegrass music it highlighted. The Recording Academy established new Grammy categories for Americana and bluegrass, suggesting that roots music carried cultural cachet in the new millennium.

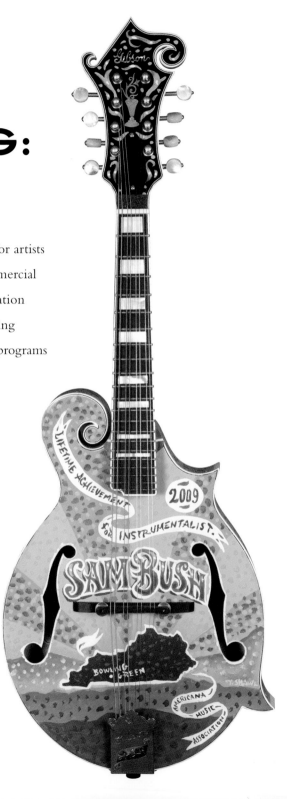

Handpainted Gibson F-5 mandolin presented to Sam Bush by the Americana Music Association in 2009 when he received their Lifetime Achievement Award for Instrumentalist.

Detail of Jim Lauderdale's stage costume, designed by Manuel

These developments proved that artists who receive relatively little attention from mainstream media still can build lasting careers. Bluegrass prodigies, such as Sam Bush and Alison Krauss, established bands that moved beyond easy genre descriptions and explored ties between disparate forms of music—while creating something distinctly their own.

Similarly, occasional collaborators Jim Lauderdale and Buddy Miller became kingpins of the Americana movement by deftly fashioning their own musical hybrids. Both crafted individual styles that used country music as a jumping off point yet brought in bluegrass, blues, rock, and soul.

Left: Stage costume designed by Manuel and worn by Jim Lauderdale.

Right: Manuscript for "Chalk," written for Buddy Miller by his wife and musical partner, Julie.

Far Right: Buddy Miller's Italian-made Wandre electric guitar.

Buddy Miller

Jim Lauderdale

Alison Krauss

The non-conformist attitudes of these and other like-minded musicians broadened country music's palette while preserving its roots. Before long, the larger music world took notice, as these musicians were invited to collaborate with such wide-ranging musicians as Robert Plant, singer-songwriter James Taylor, jazz guitarist Bill Frisell, and Grateful Dead songwriter Robert Hunter.

Right: Corset worn by Alison Krauss at the Grammy Awards, where she won five honors, including 2008 Album of the Year.

Far right: Del McCoury's 1955 Martin D-28.

Johnny Cash

Loretta Lynn

STILL CREATIVE AFTER ALL THESE YEARS:
LEGENDS AND ELDERS

A handful of country artists have had careers that endured well beyond the usual trajectory of fleeting popular success. Bill Anderson, Johnny Cash, Merle Haggard, Loretta Lynn, Willie Nelson, Dolly Parton, and Porter Wagoner inspired sustained allegiance while continuing to surprise and delight fans, even after crossing into what many would consider retirement age.

The quality of their later work added to their legacy and connected them to a younger generation. Even as country radio ignored their recordings, the veterans gained renewed attention through collaborations with younger producers and songwriters.

Cash and Lynn created startling comebacks by hooking up with rock producers, and Wagoner returned to record-making with an album produced by country stalwart Marty Stuart. Anderson co-wrote award-winning songs for hot country artists, while Nelson cut hit duets with contemporary country stars Toby Keith

This 1997 Martin D-42 JC acoustic guitar served as the prototype for a limited-edition run of two hundred Johnny Cash signature guitars.

Bill Anderson

Merle Haggard

Porter Wagoner

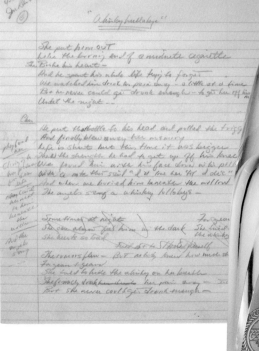

and Lee Ann Womack. Parton issued a series of successful bluegrass albums, while Haggard signed with an alternative rock label to underscore his outsider status.

At a time when most contemporary stars carefully groomed each album for massive radio play, their heroes banked more on creative growth and followed their highly individual paths.

Far left: Manuscript of Bill Anderson and Jon Randall's song "Whiskey Lullaby," written in Anderson's hand.

Left: 2005 CMA Song of the Year award for "Whiskey Lullaby."

Right: Porter Wagoner's custom-made Rich & Taylor guitar with rhinestones and sterling silver pickguard. A gift from collector and fan Mac Yasuda, it was used by Wagoner in his later years.

Detail from Brad Paisley's first electric guitar, a Sears Silvertone.

Keith Urban

COUNTRY MUSIC IN THE DIGITAL AGE:

NASHVILLE'S BRIGHT NEW STARS

The new millennium brought turmoil and change, as the music industry struggled with challenges presented by the Internet. Digital downloading reduced CD sales, and major labels signed fewer artists. Corporate consolidation tightened radio playlists, increasing competition for hit singles.

Nonetheless, country music adapted to new technology, as it always has. Artists drew from hard rock, hip-hop, and island rhythms to reach younger audiences. The Internet, satellite radio, and TV provided new ways to deliver country music. Web pages and social media such as Facebook and Twitter allowed artists to communicate directly with their followers.

Successful artists such as Kenny Chesney, Brad Paisley, and Keith Urban forged careers in tried-and-true manners: They concentrated on constant touring with exciting live shows while creating individual brands through song choices and presenting themselves to fans in singular ways.

Keith Urban's Harmony Stratotone electric guitar.

Brad Paisley

Jamey Johnson

Rascal Flatts

Miranda Lambert

Others took more modern approaches. Rascal Flatts connected with fans by incorporating modern pop-harmony vocals into country music. Carrie Underwood rode to fame as the winner of a TV talent show, while Taylor Swift used social media to enlarge her fan base and illustrate the personal side of her autobiographical songwriting.

Others adopted rebellious or outsider roles to gather fans and ulimately enter the mainstream. Miranda Lambert also got her break from a TV talent show, but she grew her stardom around her stance as an empowered, sometimes reckless woman who stood up against bad lovers and narrow social conventions. Jamey Johnson drew on the rough-hewn, rebel stances of such heroes as Waylon Jennings and Hank Williams Jr.

Jamey Johnson's Epiphone guitar.

THE SOURCES OF COUNTRY MUSIC

BY THOMAS HART BENTON

Renowned American painter Thomas Hart Benton capped his career with *The Sources of Country Music,* a remarkable mural expressing his love for many forms of American traditional music, all of which influenced the commercial art form known as country music.

Commissioned by the Country Music Hall of Fame and Museum, the 85-year-old Benton finished the mural in a carriage-house studio in Kansas City, Missouri, on January 18, 1975. "It should show the roots of the music—the sources—before there were records and stars," he said.

Benton died the day he finished the painting. The sketches and dioramas he created during the making of his artwork are now part of the archives of the Country Music Hall of Fame and Museum.

COUNTRY MUSIC HALL OF FAME

Election to the Country Music Hall of Fame is country music's highest honor. The Country Music Association created the Hall of Fame in 1961 and continues to select new members each year.

The museum's Hall of Fame Rotunda is a space of dignity and beauty that recognizes all members, with no individual given special precedence over another. The plaques representing each member are positioned randomly on the walls to ensure that everyone has a place of equal importance. The Rotunda's peaceful atmosphere inspires reverence for the deepest roots and significant figures of the music's history.

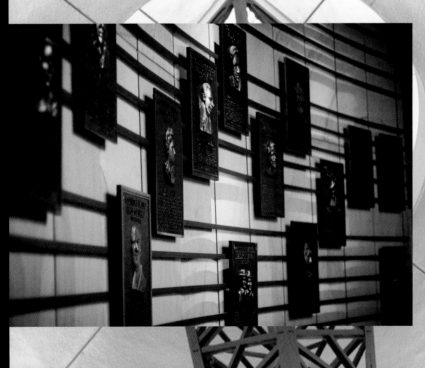

Singing "Will the Circle Be Unbroken" at the conclusion of the June 2008 Medallion Ceremony.
Left to right: Ray Walker of the Jordanaires; Little Jimmy Dickens; Reba McEntire (partially obscured); Gordon Stoker of the Jordanaires; Sonny James; Phil Balsley of the Statler Brothers; Vince Gill; Jo Walker-Meador (obscured); Tom T. Hall; Brenda Lee; Don Reid of the Statler Brothers; Ralph Emery; Earl Scruggs; Jim Foglesong; Jimmy Fortune of the Statler Brothers.

THE COUNTRY MUSIC HALL OF FAME
COUNTRY MUSIC'S GREATEST HONOR

1961 (YEAR INDUCTED)

JIMMIE RODGERS
b. September 8, 1897; d. May 26, 1933 • Birthplace: Meridian, Mississippi

His many nicknames—the Father of Country Music, the Singing Brakeman, America's Blue Yodeler—suggest not only Jimmie Rodgers's stature in American music, but also his artistic range. His highly original music—songs encompassing blues, early jazz and swing, sentimental tunes, traditional music, work chants, and yodeling—influenced generations of singers and songwriters.

FRED ROSE
b. August 24, 1898; d. December 1, 1954 • Evansville, Indiana

Drawing on a background in songwriting and performing in Chicago, New York, and Los Angeles, Fred Rose helped build the Nashville music industry. A partner in Acuff-Rose Publications, he signed Hank Williams to a songwriting contract and produced his recordings, as well as writing many pop, western, and country classics himself, including "Deed I Do," "Be Honest With Me," and "Blue Eyes Crying in the Rain."

HANK WILLIAMS
b. September 17, 1923; d. January 1, 1953 • Mount Olive, Alabama

Hank Williams, one of country music's most towering musical figures, only recorded for six years before his early death. But the power of his work set the stage for contemporary country songcraft, and he riveted audiences with his voice and charisma onstage, on recordings, on radio, and on television.

1962

ROY ACUFF
b. September 15, 1903; d. November 23, 1992 • Maynardville, Tennessee

Roy Acuff's popular updating of rural stringband music made him one of the first national stars of the Grand Ole Opry, and he remained a pillar of the famous Nashville institution a half-century later at his death. Known as the King of Country Music, he cofounded Acuff-Rose Publications, an important cornerstone of the Nashville music industry.

1963
(No Inductions)

1964

TEX RITTER
b. January 12, 1905; d. January 2, 1974 • Panola County, Texas

Tex Ritter came to western music honestly, immersing himself in cowboy songs while growing up in Texas. His deep voice and theatrical sensibility led him to star in Broadway musicals and Hollywood films. He later helped solidify Nashville's reputation by becoming a Grand Ole Opry star, radio host, and CMA president.

1965

ERNEST TUBB
b. February 9, 1914; d. September 6, 1984 • near Crisp, Texas

With his distinctive baritone voice and laconic style, Ernest Tubb became one of country music's first honky-tonk stars. He helped usher in the electric guitar as a primary country instrument, and his focus on good musicianship, non-stop touring, and helping up-and-coming artists made him a beloved and influential figure.

Cindy Walker at the 1997 CMA Awards.

1966

EDDY ARNOLD

b. May 15, 1918; d. May 8, 2008 • Henderson, Tennessee

Eddy Arnold, with his smooth voice and refined manner, personified country music's adaptation to a modern, more urban world and its transition from folk-based sounds to pop-influenced ones. By scoring Top Ten hits from the 1940s to 1980, he enjoyed one of American music's most enduring music careers.

JIM DENNY

b. February 28, 1911; d. August 27, 1963 • Buffalo Valley, Tennessee

Longtime manager of the Grand Ole Opry Artists Service, Jim Denny eventually left Nashville's WSM to become one of the most successful talent agents and song publishers in country music history. He formed Cedarwood Publishing Company in 1953 with Webb Pierce, and he later owned several radio stations.

GEORGE D. HAY

b. November 9, 1895; d. May 8, 1968 • Attica, Indiana

Founder of WSM's Grand Ole Opry, George D. Hay played a vital role in commercializing country music and helping form its rural image in its early years. Known as "the Solemn Old Judge," he named the Opry in an impromptu on-air statement in 1927 and long served as its chief announcer, publicist, and spokesman.

UNCLE DAVE MACON

b. October 7, 1870; d. March 22, 1952 • Smart Station, Tennessee

An early star of the Grand Ole Opry, Uncle Dave Macon ranks among the most colorful figures in American entertainment history. A skilled banjo player, strong singer, and mirthful comedian, the master showman bridged the vaudeville tradition of the nineteenth century with the commercial music that followed the advent of radio and phonographs.

1967

RED FOLEY
b. June 17, 1910; d. September 19, 1968 • Blue Lick, Kentucky

Singer Red Foley helped spread country music's popularity through recordings, concerts, and high-profile roles on radio and television programs in Chicago, Cincinnati, Nashville, and Springfield, Missouri. He created classic hits with sentimental songs ("Old Shep"), boogie tunes ("Tennessee Saturday Night"), pop-swing ("Chattanoogie Shoe Shine Boy"), and gospel ("Peace in the Valley").

J. L. FRANK
b. April 15, 1900; d. May 4, 1952 • Limestone County, Alabama

Joseph Lee "J. L." Frank became the first major country music promoter and manager in Nashville. After working in Chicago booking Gene Autry, Frank eventually relocated to Nashville and promoted shows starring Roy Acuff, Eddy Arnold, Pee Wee King, Minnie Pearl, Ernest Tubb, and other Grand Ole Opry stars.

JIM REEVES
b. August 20, 1923; d. July 31, 1964 • Panola County, Texas

The velvet-smooth baritone of Jim Reeves made him one of country music's most distinctive singers and one of the biggest crossover stars of his era. After enjoying hits in Louisiana, Reeves moved to Nashville and joined the Grand Ole Opry. His intimate vocals complemented the lush, sophisticated production style known as the Nashville Sound.

STEVE SHOLES
b. February 12, 1911; d. April 22, 1968 • Washington, D.C.

Record executive and producer Steve Sholes helped shepherd country music's growth and publicize its cultural importance in the years following World War II. He signed Eddy Arnold, Chet Atkins, the Browns, Pee Wee King, Elvis Presley, Jim Reeves, and Hank Snow to RCA Records, and he gave Atkins his start as a leading Nashville producer and RCA executive.

1968

BOB WILLS
b. March 6, 1905; d. May 13, 1975 • Kosse, Texas

Bob Wills is synonymous with western swing. A bandleader, showman, fiddler, singer, and songwriter, he helped create and popularize a form of dance music that blended big band jazz, blues, traditional fiddle tunes, mariachi music, and ragtime. His band, the Texas Playboys, showcased several of country music's most influential musicians.

1969

GENE AUTRY
b. September 29, 1907; d. October 2, 1998 • Tioga, Texas

Hollywood's first famous singing cowboy, Gene Autry ranked as the best-selling country artist from the Depression through World War II. Through his screen roles and as a radio show host, he introduced a romanticized form of western music to the nation. A successful businessman, he was a longtime owner of the Los Angeles Angels baseball team.

1970

CARTER FAMILY
Formed 1927 in Clinch Valley, Virginia

"The first family of country music," the Carter Family ranks among the genre's most popular early acts. A.P. Carter, his wife Sara Carter, and her cousin Maybelle Carter popularized an influential form of harmony singing, and Maybelle's guitar-picking style proved so important that it became known as the "Carter scratch."

BILL MONROE
b. September 13, 1911; d. September 9, 1996 • Rosine, Kentucky

The Father of Bluegrass, as Bill Monroe was known, aptly describes his role as the founder of an intense, tightly arranged, harmony-rich form of stringband music laced with blues and gospel influences. A powerful mandolinist, Monroe sang in a tight-throated tenor that defined the genre's high, lonesome sound.

1971

ART SATHERLEY
b. October 19, 1889; d. February 10, 1986 • Bristol, England

Art Satherley ranks among early country music's most important record executives. A producer, talent scout, salesman, and manufacturing supervisor, he sought out country and blues artists, working with Roy Acuff, Gene Autry, Spade Cooley, Vernon Dalhart, Al Dexter, Red Foley, Bill Monroe, Tex Ritter, Bob Wills, and other leading country music artists.

1972

JIMMIE DAVIS
b. September 11, 1899; d. November 5, 2000 • Beech Springs, Louisiana

In the 1930s and 1940s, Jimmie Davis's smooth vocal approach helped popularize country music beyond its rural southern audience. His best-selling songs—including "You Are My Sunshine" and "Nobody's Darling but Mine"—not only made him a star but also helped him win roles in Hollywood films and two terms as governor of Louisiana.

1973

CHET ATKINS
b. June 20, 1924; d. June 30, 2001 • Luttrell, Tennessee

No single country instrumentalist achieved the acclaim and respect that Chet Atkins did. His innovative guitar work influenced country, rock, and jazz musicians. He also made his mark as a record producer and RCA executive, running the label's Nashville office from 1955 to 1973 and producing dozens of classic country hits.

PATSY CLINE
b. September 8, 1932; d. March 5, 1963 • Winchester, Virginia

Although popular in her time, Patsy Cline achieved iconic status after a plane crash tragically ended her life. Her rich alto voice, with its impeccable phrasing and emotional expressiveness, has come to set the standard for vocalists in country music and beyond. A 1985 biographical film, *Sweet Dreams*, helped spread her fame.

1974

OWEN BRADLEY
b. October 21, 1915; d. January 7, 1998 • Westmoreland, Tennessee

Owen Bradley was an architect of the Nashville Sound, built one of the first entertainment businesses on what became Music Row, and produced hits with more than a half dozen members of the Country Music Hall of Fame. Bradley ran Decca Records' Nashville division from 1958 to 1976, after Decca was absorbed by MCA.

PEE WEE KING
b. February 18, 1914; d. March 7, 2000 • Milwaukee, Wisconsin

Pee Wee King became a country music star while including waltzes, polkas, and western music in his repertoire. His band, the Golden West Cowboys, at various times included such important country music figures as Eddy Arnold, Cowboy Copas, Minnie Pearl, Redd Stewart, and Ernest Tubb. He also co-wrote the crossover classic "Tennessee Waltz."

1975

MINNIE PEARL
b. October 25, 1912; d. January 7, 1998 • Centerville, Tennessee

Minnie Pearl was the undisputed queen of country comedy. She became a Grand Ole Opry fixture as a flirtatious spinster who joked about her rural hometown, Grinder Switch. Her trademarks included unstylish gingham dresses, a straw hat adorned with a $1.98 price tag, and her cheerful greeting, "How-dee! I'm just so proud to be here!"

1976

PAUL COHEN
b. November 10, 1908; d. April 1, 1970 • Chicago, Illinois

Paul Cohen, head of Decca Records' country department from the mid-1940s to 1958, played a major role in Nashville's emergence as a country music recording capital. Based in New York, Cohen began recording Decca stars Red Foley and Ernest Tubb in Nashville by 1947, when he hired producer Owen Bradley to help him oversee Decca's country music roster.

Eddy Arnold is presented with his Country Music Hall of Fame plaque, 1966.
Future Hall of Fame member Jo Walker-Meador is at far right.

KITTY WELLS

b. August 30, 1919 • Nashville, Tennessee

Kitty Wells was thirty-three and contemplating retirement in 1952 when her breakthrough hit, "It Wasn't God Who Made Honky Tonk Angels," made her a star. Her piercing, intensely honest vocal style and the down-to-earth themes of her songs resonated with audiences and broke barriers for female country singers.

1977

MERLE TRAVIS

b. November 29, 1917; d. October 20, 1983 • Rosewood, Kentucky

A backwoods renaissance man, Merle Travis was an innovative guitarist, songwriter, and vocalist, as well as a guitar designer, cartoonist, and author. He wrote many country hits, including "Sixteen Tons" and "Divorce Me C.O.D.," and profoundly influenced several generations of musicians, including Chet Atkins.

1978

GRANDPA JONES

b. October 20, 1913; d. February 19, 1998 • Niagara, Kentucky

An exuberant banjoist, vocalist, and comedian, Grandpa Jones was a dedicated champion of old-time music. He continued to play clawhammer banjo when others shifted toward the three-finger style popularized by Earl Scruggs, and his roles on the Grand Ole Opry, *Hee Haw*, and in gospel quartets kept country music connected to its early roots.

1979

HUBERT LONG

b. December 3, 1923; d. September 7, 1972 • Poteet, Texas

A leading Nashville talent promoter, artist manager, and music publisher, Hubert Long was a top country music executive in the 1950s and 1960s. The Hubert Long Agency became one of Nashville's first independent talent agencies, and he was a founding board member of the Country Music Association and the Country Music Hall of Fame and Museum.

Country Music Hall of Fame members Porter Wagoner, Jim Foglesong, and Kris Kristofferson at the 2003 Medallion Ceremony.

HANK SNOW

b. May 9, 1914; d. December 20, 1999 • Brooklyn, Nova Scotia, Canada

Hank Snow combined a distinctive vocal style and songwriting gifts to establish himself as one of the biggest country stars in the years following World War II. An accomplished guitarist as well, he experimented with Latin rhythms, jazz, blues, Hawaiian music, and gospel songs, giving them all an individual touch of his own.

1980

JOHNNY CASH
b. February 26, 1932; d. September 12, 2003 • Kingsland, Arkansas

An international ambassador for country music, Johnny Cash connected with prisoners and presidents, and with rebels and religious figures. He developed a starkly minimalist sound with his band, the Tennessee Two, which framed his deep, authoritative voice, leading to an enduring career including success as an actor, author, and network TV host.

CONNIE B. GAY
b. August 22, 1914; d. December 4, 1989 • Lizard Lick, North Carolina

Dubbed country music's Media Magician, Connie B. Gay became a leading country music entrepreneur. Working out of Washington, D.C., in the 1950s and 1960s, Gay organized radio, TV, and stage shows that helped turn rural-based country music into an all-American form of modern entertainment.

SONS OF THE PIONEERS
Formed 1933 in Los Angeles, California

America's premier western vocal group, the Sons of the Pioneers drew on cowboy themes and featured three-part harmonies and stellar instrumental work. Original members included Roy Rogers, who went on to solo fame as a singer and actor, as well as ace songwriters Bob Nolan and Tim Spencer, and brothers Hugh and Karl Farr.

1981

VERNON DALHART
b. April 6, 1883; d. September 14, 1948 • Jefferson, Texas

Vernon Dalhart, an operatically trained singer, became one of the most productive and versatile performers in early country music. His 1924 recording of "The Wreck of the Old '97" coupled with "The Prisoner's Song" is credited as country music's first million seller. His clear diction helped make down-home country material accessible to broad audiences, both rural and urban.

GRANT TURNER
b. May 17, 1912; d. October 19, 1991 • Baird, Texas

Grant Turner, known as the Voice of the Grand Ole Opry, served on the show's announcing staff for forty-seven years and became a broadcasting icon. Beloved for his warm manner, careful diction, and ingratiating personality, Turner was one of three original members elected to the Country Disc Jockey Hall of Fame.

1982

LEFTY FRIZZELL
b. March 31, 1928; d. July 19, 1975 • Corsicana, Texas

Lefty Frizzell, known for his vowel-bending phrasing and intimate vocal tone, ranks among the most influential performers in country music history. His distinctive style helped shape the artistry of Merle Haggard, George Jones, George Strait, Randy Travis, and Keith Whitley. Frizzell enjoyed a run of top hits in the 1950s and continued recording until his death.

ROY HORTON
b. November 5, 1914; d. September 23, 2003 • Broad Top, Pennsylvania

After performing in the Hilltoppers with his brother Vaughan, Roy Horton spent forty years as an important executive with Peer-Southern Music, a top country music publishing company. A CMA stalwart, he developed the catalogs of the Carter Family, Ted Daffan, Jimmie Davis, Bill Monroe, Jimmie Rodgers, Floyd Tillman, and other country greats.

MARTY ROBBINS
b. September 26, 1925; d. December 8, 1982 • near Glendale, Arizona

Marty Robbins achieved success as a recording artist, stage performer, songwriter, TV program host, actor, author, and stock car racer. The versatile singer applied his supple voice to country, gospel, Hawaiian, pop, rockabilly, and western material. A fan favorite, his midnight performances on the Grand Ole Opry became a long-running tradition.

1983

LITTLE JIMMY DICKENS
b. December 19, 1920 • Bolt, West Virginia

Little Jimmy Dickens's big voice and brassy style—paired with his physical stature of four feet, eleven inches—made him a favorite with country fans. Starting in 1949, he first made his reputation with a string of novelty songs, but soon proved to be a versatile entertainer who delivered tear-filled ballads and rockabilly tunes with equal effectiveness.

1984

RALPH PEER
b. May 22, 1892; d. January 19, 1960 • Kansas City, Missouri

Ralph Peer was the most prominent businessman in early country music. Indeed, his impact on the larger popular music industry—as a pioneer in recording, music publishing, and artist management—is incalculable. Among other accomplishments, he discovered the Carter Family and Jimmie Rodgers and steered the their rise to prominence.

FLOYD TILLMAN
b. December 8, 1914; d. August 22, 2003 • Ryan, Oklahoma

In the 1930s and 1940s, singer-songwriter Floyd Tillman contributed to the rise of western swing and honky-tonk music while penning country standards. His songwriting catalog includes early crossover hits, such as "It Makes No Difference Now," "I Love You So Much It Hurts," and "Slippin' Around."

1985

FLATT & SCRUGGS
Formed 1948 in Nashville, Tennessee

Flatt & Scruggs helped popularize bluegrass music in the 1950s and 1960s. Singer-guitarist Lester Flatt and banjoist extraordinaire Earl Scruggs joined Bill Monroe & His Blue Grass Boys in 1945, leaving in 1948 and forming their own band soon after. Their syndicated TV show and other work on TV and movie soundtracks spread their fame worldwide.

Country Music Hall of Fame inductees Jean Shepard, Bobby Braddock, and Reba McEntire, 2011.

1986

THE DUKE OF PADUCAH
b. May 12, 1901; d. June 20, 1986 • DeSoto, Missouri

Benjamin "Whitey" Ford was a leading country comedian from the 1930s to the 1950s. He acquired his stage moniker, the Duke of Paducah, while broadcasting on St. Louis radio station KWK. He helped organize the *Renfro Valley Barn Dance* and starred for years on the Grand Ole Opry's network segment.

WESLEY ROSE
b. February 11, 1918; d. April 26, 1990 • Chicago, Illinois

Wesley Rose joined Acuff-Rose Publications in 1945 at the invitation of his father, Fred Rose, and later became one of the world's top music-publishing executives. After his father's death in 1954, Rose became the firm's president, as well as head of Hickory Records. He later launched the Acuff-Rose Artists Corporation and became a successful record producer.

1987
ROD BRASFIELD
b. August 22, 1910; d. September 12, 1958 • Smithville, Mississippi

From 1947 to 1958, Grand Ole Opry star Rod Brasfield was a premier country music comedian. His trademark baggy suit, button shoes, beat-up hat, rubbery face, and clacking false teeth would have audiences laughing before he spoke. Brasfield also starred in the 1957 film *A Face in the Crowd*.

1988
LORETTA LYNN
b. April 14, 1932 • Butcher Holler, Kentucky

Despite growing up in poverty, marrying in her mid-teens, and having four children by age twenty, Loretta Lynn became one of country's most popular performers. Assertive, autobiographical songs, including "You Ain't Woman Enough" and "Don't Come Home a-Drinkin' (with Lovin' on Your Mind)," broke ground for female singer-songwriters. Her 1978 autobiography, *Coal Miner's Daughter*, became an award-winning film.

ROY ROGERS
b. November 5, 1911; d. July 6, 1998 • Cincinnati, Ohio

Roy Rogers earned the title King of the Cowboys by succeeding Gene Autry as America's most popular western film star. Before beginning his movie career and starring with wife Dale Evans on film and TV, Rogers was a founding member of western vocal group the Sons of the Pioneers.

1989
JACK STAPP
b. December 8, 1912; d. December 20, 1980 • Nashville, Tennessee

Jack Stapp made country music history in two executive posts: As WSM radio's program director from 1939 to 1957, he signed such artists as Red Foley, Carl Smith, Hank Snow, and Hank Williams to the Grand Ole Opry. In 1951 Stapp also founded the enormously successful Tree Publishing Company, later bought by Sony Music.

CLIFFIE STONE
b. March 1, 1917; d. January 17, 1998 • Stockton, California

Over six decades, Cliffie Stone contributed to country music as a radio and TV personality, recording artist, bass player, record producer, talent scout, song publisher, and artist manager. All of those roles made him a pivotal figure in the development of California's post-war country music scene.

HANK THOMPSON
b. September 3, 1925; d. November 6, 2007 • Waco, Texas

Hank Thompson created a distinctive blend of honky-tonk and western swing that gave him a lengthy career and helped keep these traditions alive during the rise of rock & roll and country's experimentation with rock and pop. Between 1948 and 1974, Thompson scored twenty-eight Top Ten hits and continued to chart into the 1980s.

1990
TENNESSEE ERNIE FORD
b. February 13, 1919; d. October 17, 1991 • Bristol, Tennessee

With a resonant baritone and good-natured humor, Tennessee Ernie Ford gained success as a recording artist, actor, comedian, and TV host. Besides releasing crossover hits such as "Sixteen Tons," Ford recorded a series of popular gospel albums. He hosted several NBC-TV programs, including a game show and his own variety series.

1991
BOUDLEAUX AND FELICE BRYANT
Married September 5, 1945, in Milwaukee, Wisconsin

Husband and wife Boudleaux and Felice Bryant were among the first in Nashville to make a full-time career of songwriting. They wrote some of the most memorable songs of the 1950s and 1960s, including many hits for the Everly Brothers, such as "Bye Bye Love," "Wake Up, Little Susie," and "All I Have to Do Is Dream."

1992
GEORGE JONES
b. September 12, 1931 • Saratoga, Texas

George Jones's wide vocal range and his emotive way with lyrics made him one of the most admired country artists in history and a successor of such masters as Hank Williams and Lefty Frizzell. His drama-filled life, with its trials and triumphs, gave his work a realistic feel that cemented his connection with fans.

FRANCES PRESTON
b. August 27, 1928; d. June 13, 2012 • Nashville, Tennessee

Frances Preston rose from working as a receptionist at WSM radio to become one of the most important music business leaders in America. In 1958, her contacts and professionalism led BMI to ask her to open its southern regional office in Nashville. By 1986, she was BMI's president and CEO, based in New York. She retired from BMI in 2004.

1993
WILLIE NELSON
b. April 30, 1933 • Abbott, Texas

One of country music's most versatile and enduring singer-songwriters, Nelson recorded twenty-one #1 hits between 1962 and 1993. But that's only part of the story, as Nelson's restless creativity and boundless energy have resulted in a career that has embraced nearly every genre of American music and featured collaborations with dozens of other artists.

1994
MERLE HAGGARD
b. April 6, 1937 • Bakersfield, California

With the possible exception of Hank Williams, Merle Haggard is country music's most influential singer-songwriter. He is also one of the genre's most versatile artists, mining honky-tonk, blues, jazz, pop, and folk, yet making all his recordings personal and distinctly his own. He also helped establish Bakersfield, California, as an important country music center.

1995
ROGER MILLER
b. January 2, 1936; d. October 25, 1992 • Fort Worth, Texas

Roger Miller left a musical legacy of astonishing depth and range. First finding success as a songwriter, he exploded in popularity as a Grammy-winning performer in the 1960s with the clever, witty crossover hits "Dang Me," "King of the Road," and "Chug-a-Lug." He won a 1985 Tony Award for his musical score for *Big River*.

1996
PATSY MONTANA
b. October 30, 1908; d. May 3, 1996 • Hope, Arkansas

Patsy Montana's 1935 recording of "I Wanna Be a Cowboy's Sweetheart" was the first female solo recording to become a runaway hit. With a sparkling voice, spirited yodeling, and signature cowgirl outfits, she sang of love, independence, and the romance of the West—appealing to Depression Era fans in need of cheerful entertainment.

BUCK OWENS
b. August 12, 1929; d. March 25, 2006 • Sherman, Texas

Singer, songwriter, and guitarist Buck Owens ruled country music in the 1960s. His many hits—energetic, guitar-driven, danceable—helped define the West Coast country sound. He later became a fixture on television as co-host of the long-running syndicated program *Hee Haw*. A highly successful businessman, he oversaw a variety of profitable ventures.

Presentation of Country Music Hall of Fame plaques at the 1973 CMA Awards.

Left to right: Tex Ritter, Chet Atkins, and Roy Acuff.

RAY PRICE
b. January 12, 1926 • Perryville, Texas

Ray Price ranks among country music's most important innovators and one of its most enduring artists. He changed the sound of country music from the late 1950s forward by developing a rhythmic form of honky-tonk that has been a staple of country music ever since. He later recorded lushly orchestrated pop-country ballads that also broke new ground.

1997

HARLAN HOWARD
b. September 8, 1927; d. March 3, 2002 • Detroit, Michigan

Harlan Howard stands as the archetype of the professional Nashville songwriter. Arriving in Nashville in 1960 after penning hits for Buck Owens and Charlie Walker, he approached songwriting as a daily job and wrote dozens of country classics across the decades, from Patsy Cline's "I Fall to Pieces" to the Judds' "Why Not Me."

BRENDA LEE
b. December 11, 1944 • Atlanta, Georgia

Brenda Lee ranks among America's most talented singers, and her immense success as a pop artist, along with Elvis Presley and the Everly Brothers, helped make Nashville an all-purpose recording center. As rock overtook pop on the charts, Lee turned to country music in the 1970s and gained hits into the 1980s.

CINDY WALKER
b. July 20, 1918; d. November 12, 2008 • Mart, Texas

Cindy Walker became one of country music's finest songwriters through a knack to tailor songs for a diverse list of stylists, including Eddy Arnold, Gene Autry, Hank Snow, and Bob Wills. Her Top Ten hits spanned a half century, ranging from "Cherokee Maiden" to "You Don't Know Me" to "Dream Baby (How Long Must I Dream)."

Brenda Lee with her Country Music Hall of Fame plaque, 1997.

1998

GEORGE MORGAN
b. June 29, 1924; d. July 7, 1975 • Waverly, Tennessee

George Morgan's smooth tenor made him a fixture on the Grand Ole Opry for decades. In 1949, he had five singles simultaneously in the country Top Ten, including his signature hit, "Candy Kisses." Morgan hosted a Nashville TV show in the 1950s and, in 1973, introduced his daughter Lorrie Morgan for her Grand Ole Opry debut.

ELVIS PRESLEY
b. January 8, 1935; d. August 16, 1977 • Tupelo, Missouri

Elvis Presley remains rock & roll's most important figure, but he initially set out to be a country singer, and several of his early songs came from the genre. He later recorded country music, and his impact on the genre was immense, helping it move from a regional phenomenon to national status.

E.W. "BUD" WENDELL
b. August 17, 1927 • Akron, Ohio

Bud Wendell advanced country music in several executive roles: longtime manager of the Grand Ole Opry; president and CEO of the company that owned the Opry and the Opryland hotel and theme park; and developer of the cable TV networks TNN and CMT. He also was board chairman of the Country Music Hall of Fame and Museum for many years.

TAMMY WYNETTE
b. May 5, 1942; d. April 6, 1998 • Itawamba County, Mississippi

On record and on stage, Tammy Wynette paired southern dignity with country grit. A former hairdresser, she cultivated a glamorous appearance and sang with an omnipresent tear and twang in her voice. Her songs dealt with the romantic ideals and difficulties of family-oriented women, both as a soloist and in her duets with third husband George Jones.

1999
JOHNNY BOND
b. June 1, 1915; d. June 12, 1978 • Enville, Oklahoma

Johnny Bond was an important western music songwriter and performer. He composed hundreds of songs, including such classics as "Cimarron," "I Wonder Where You Are Tonight," and "Tomorrow Never Comes." He also was an actor, author, a regular on California-based TV and radio programs, and a music publisher with business partner Tex Ritter.

DOLLY PARTON
b. January 19, 1946 • Locust Ridge, Tennessee

Dolly Parton's striking artistry and image helped revolutionize the world of country music for female performers. In 1967, she had her first solo hit and became Porter Wagoner's duet partner on recordings, on stage, and on his syndicated TV series. Going solo in 1974, she recorded pop hits, starred on TV and in films, and opened an East Tennessee theme park.

CONWAY TWITTY
b. September 1, 1933; d. June 5, 1993 • Friars Point, Mississippi

During his lifetime, Conway Twitty had more #1 records than any country artist to that point. A diverse stylist and significant songwriter, his first success came with the 1958 pop hit "It's Only Make Believe" before turning to country music in the 1960s. Twitty also recorded a series of famous duets with Loretta Lynn.

2000
CHARLEY PRIDE
b. March 18, 1938 • Sledge, Mississippi

Although country music's only black superstar, Charley Pride would be a legend no matter what his ethnicity. His southern baritone voice first hit country radio in 1966, and he continued enjoying hits for more than twenty years. Pride also proved to be an astute businessman, investing in real estate and banking from his home in Dallas.

FARON YOUNG
b. February 25, 1932; d. December 10, 1996 • Shreveport, Louisiana

From the 1950s through the 1970s, Faron Young was a leading country star and one of the genre's most colorful personalities. He recorded hits as a honky-tonker and as a sensitive balladeer, and, on the side, he became a magazine publisher and real estate investor.

2001

BILL ANDERSON

b. November 1, 1937 • Columbia, South Carolina

Among country music's most successful singer-songwriters, Bill Anderson recorded thirty-seven Top Ten singles between 1960 and 1978, and he has written country hits for more than fifty years. His breathy, conversational tenor earned him the nickname "Whisperin' Bill." In addition, he has worked as an actor, fronted a syndicated TV music program, and hosted TV game shows.

DELMORE BROTHERS

Formed circa 1931 in Elkmont, Alabama

The Delmore Brothers, Alton and Rabon, were arguably the most musically sophisticated and technically proficient of the many great brother duos of the 1930s and 1940s. Their soft, pliant harmony, dazzling guitar work, love of blues, and well-crafted songs endeared them to generations of fans. Several of their hits—including "Brown's Ferry Blues" and "Blues Stay Away from Me"—became country standards.

EVERLY BROTHERS

Formed circa 1954 in Kentucky

The Everly Brothers, Don and Phil, were one of popular music's most successful acts between 1957 and 1962. They also were important to Nashville, as they were the city's first consistently successful rock & roll act. Their management and songs came from Nashville, and they recorded with local studio musicians. They split in 1973 and reunited ten years later.

DON GIBSON

b. April 3, 1928; d. November 17, 2003 • Shelby, North Carolina

Masterful songwriter and performer Don Gibson composed three of country music's most famous songs: "Sweet Dreams," "Oh Lonesome Me," and "I Can't Stop Loving You." He also released more than seventy charted singles between 1956 and 1980, and his recordings, produced by Chet Atkins, helped define the musical style known as the Nashville Sound.

Kitty Wells with her Country Music Hall of Fame plaque, 1976.

HOMER & JETHRO

Formed 1936 in Knoxville, Tennessee

Famous for their song satires, dry comic delivery, and instrumental virtuosity, Homer & Jethro (Henry "Homer" Haynes and Kenneth "Jethro" Burns) were country music's most beloved comedy act. Their success took them from radio barn dances to network television variety shows, urban nightclubs, and Las Vegas showrooms.

WAYLON JENNINGS

b. June 15, 1937; d. February 13, 2002 • Littlefield, Texas

Waylon Jennings worked in radio, played in Buddy Holly's band, roomed with Johnny Cash, and acted in a 1967 film, *Nashville Rebel*, before he became a music star. Jennings grew into a musical hero in the early 1970s when he assumed artistic control of his albums and helped create what became known as the Outlaw movement.

JORDANAIRES

Formed 1948 in Springfield, Missouri

Nashville's premier background vocal group, the Jordanaires established themselves as a gospel quartet before they won fame for their studio work. Elvis Presley invited the group to back him starting in 1956, which led to a long association with Presley and a lengthy run as a renowned harmony act, on their own and behind other vocalists.

DON LAW

b. February 24, 1902; d. December 20, 1982 • London, England

The head of Columbia Records' country music division from 1952 to 1967, Don Law was one of the most successful producers in the annals of country music. He worked with stars Johnny Cash, Lefty Frizzell, Johnny Horton, Ray Price, and Carl Smith—gaining their respect for letting them forge their own sounds.

George Strait and Bill Anderson, 2007 Medallion Ceremony.

LOUVIN BROTHERS

Formed 1942 in Henegar, Alabama

Ira and Charlie Louvin of the Louvin Brothers were the link between early brother duets such as the Delmore Brothers and the more modern Everly Brothers. Moreover, the Louvins' stratospheric vocal interplay made them one of country music's most influential acts of any era. Charlie Louvin established a solo career after splitting from Ira, who died in 1965.

KEN NELSON

b. January 19, 1911; d. January 6, 2008 • Caledonia, Minnesota

Ken Nelson handled A&R for the country division of Capitol Records from 1951 to 1969, helping give country music a national presence after World War II. Nelson was considered an artist-friendly record producer, encouraging artists such as Merle Haggard, Wanda Jackson, Buck Owens, and Jerry Reed to develop styles of their own.

SAM PHILLIPS

b. January 5, 1923; d. July 30, 2004 • Florence, Alabama

One of American music's most important figures, Sam Phillips founded Sun Records and introduced the world to Johnny Cash, Jerry Lee Lewis, Roy Orbison, Carl Perkins, Elvis Presley, and Charlie Rich. By seeking artists with style and vision, and by recording them as raw as possible, he captured distinctive sounds that launched legendary careers.

WEBB PIERCE

b. August 8, 1921; d. February 24, 1991 • West Monroe, Louisiana

Webb Pierce was one of country music's biggest stars in the 1950s— and one of its most flamboyant, with his flashy Nudie-tailored suits and custom cars. Pierce's high, piercing tenor gave him an instantly identifiable voice, and his knack for recognizing a good country song led to thirteen #1 singles in the 1950s.

2002

BILL CARLISLE

b. December 19, 1908; d. March 17, 2003 • Wakefield, Kentucky

A top showman and talented songwriter, Bill Carlisle joined the first generation of country performers in the 1920s and was still performing his mix of blues-influenced, old-time country and novelty songs in the twenty-first century. He first performed with his brother Cliff, and for more than fifty years led a family group, the Carlisles.

PORTER WAGONER

b. August 12, 1927; d. October 28, 2007 • Howell County, Missouri

Porter Wagoner became one of country music's most enduring and recognizable stars. Wagoner's achievements included eighty-one chart records—including several country standards. He served as a beloved TV program host and an expert showman easily identified by his blond pompadour, rhinestone suits, and down-home humor. After Roy Acuff's death, Wagoner served as the unofficial spokesman for the Grand Ole Opry.

2003

FLOYD CRAMER

b. October 27, 1933; d. December 31, 1997 • Shreveport, Louisiana

Floyd Cramer became one of the busiest musicians in Nashville once the piano became an integral instrument in country arrangements starting in the late 1950s. He popularized the slip-note technique, a popular feature of country recordings, and his tasteful playing was heard on his own instrumental hits, such as "Last Date" and "San Antonio Rose."

CARL SMITH

b. March 15, 1927; d. January 16, 2010 • Maynardville, Tennessee

Carl Smith stands as one of country's most popular hitmakers in the 1950s and 1960s. Influenced by Roy Acuff and Hank Williams, the tall, handsome singer developed a hard-edged sound that he presented with easy confidence. He co-hosted the nationally televised *Five Star Jubilee* program and for five years hosted a Canadian program, *Carl Smith's Country Music Hall.*

2004

JIM FOGLESONG

b. July 26, 1922 • Lundale, West Virginia

As a producer and record label executive, Jim Foglesong advanced the careers of many country acts while inspiring associates with his high ethical standards. After success as a pop producer, Foglesong moved to Nashville in 1970 as A&R chief for Dot Records. He later headed the local offices of the ABC-Dot, MCA, and Capitol labels.

KRIS KRISTOFFERSON

b. June 22, 1936 • Brownsville, Texas

Few songwriters have exerted more influence on country music or have been as successful beyond the limits of Music Row as Kris Kristofferson. Since the 1960s, Kristofferson has excelled as a recording artist and Hollywood actor, and, as a songwriter, he established standards that continue to set the bar for others in his field.

2005

ALABAMA

Formed 1973 in Fort Payne, Alabama

Few bands have affected country music's success as much as Alabama. The family-based act—Randy Owen on vocals and guitar, Jeff Cook on guitar, Teddy Gentry on bass, Mark Herndon on drums—had thirty-two #1 country hits, sold millions of albums, and proved that a self-contained band could achieve top sales and status in country music.

DeFORD BAILEY

b. December 14, 1899; d. July 2, 1982 • Smith County, Tennessee

DeFord Bailey was the first black star of the Grand Ole Opry and one of its most popular early performers. A harmonica specialist, Bailey recorded for Brunswick and Victor, the latter marking the first recording sessions held in Nashville by a major label. He also toured widely, despite the Jim Crow laws of the time.

Little Jimmy Dickens and Carl Smith at the 2003 Medallion Ceremony.

GLEN CAMPBELL

b. April 22, 1936 • Delight, Arkansas

A gifted singer and guitarist, Glen Campbell rose to stardom with a string of pop-country hits in the 1960s and 1970s. At his peak, Campbell hosted *The Glen Campbell Goodtime Hour*, a CBS-TV variety show, from 1968 to 1972. He also starred in several movies, including *True Grit* with John Wayne.

2006

HAROLD BRADLEY

b. January 2, 1926 • Nashville, Tennessee

The "Dean of the Nashville Session Guitarists," Harold Bradley played his first recording session in 1946, with Pee Wee King. Since then, he has played on hundreds of hit recordings, for everyone from Eddy Arnold and Red Foley to Elvis Presley and Roy Orbison. He headed the Nashville Chapter of the American Federation of Musicians from 1991 to 2008.

SONNY JAMES

b. May 1, 1929 • Hackleburg, Alabama

Sonny James has enjoyed one of country music's most distinguished careers. Between 1953 and 1983, he amassed seventy-two chart records, twenty-three of which went to #1. Known as the Southern Gentleman for his gracious manner, James enjoyed his greatest success singing romantic ballads. He also worked as a producer, helping Marie Osmond with her #1 crossover hit, "Paper Roses."

GEORGE STRAIT

b. May 18, 1952 • Poteet, Texas

George Strait arrived as a Texas traditionalist amid a contemporary country scene in which pop-crossover sounds prevailed. Bucking convention, he went on to become one of the most successful, enduring, and influential recording artists of his time. He has had more than ninety chart hits and more #1s than any other artist in country music history.

2007

RALPH EMERY

b. March 10, 1933 • McEwen, Tennessee

Ralph Emery ranks as one of the most famous radio and TV personalities in country music. The longtime WSM radio deejay hosted the popular TNN prime-time talk show, *Nashville Now*, as well as long-running syndicated programs (*Pop Goes the Country, Nashville Alive*) and a daily morning Nashville TV program, *The Ralph Emery Show*.

VINCE GILL

b. April 12, 1957 • Norman, Oklahoma

Vince Gill is one of the most awarded country stars of his era, thanks to his aching tenor voice, his songwriting skills, and his virtuoso guitar chops. Besides registering a long string of hits, he hosted the CMA Awards from 1992 to 2003, and his easygoing demeanor and devotion to charitable causes have made him one of country music's best-liked insiders.

MEL TILLIS

b. August 8, 1932 • Pahokee, Florida

Mel Tillis parlayed his success as a respected Nashville songwriter in the 1950s and 1960s into a substantial recording and touring career that flourished in the 1970s and beyond. A chronic stutterer, Tillis used this challenge to enhance an affable, down-home comic persona that resulted in film roles and a strong TV presence.

2008

TOM T. HALL

b. May 25, 1936 • Olive Hill, Kentucky

Tom T. Hall was among the leading songwriters who, in the 1960s and 1970s, imbued country music with a new level of lyric and thematic sophistication and social consciousness, while maintaining the music's inherent rusticity and simplicity of form. Known as "The Storyteller," Hall flourished as a recording artist with original, poignant, sometimes sardonic musical slices of life.

EMMYLOU HARRIS

b. April 2, 1947 • Birmingham, Alabama

Emmylou Harris has stretched beyond the conventional parameters of country, bluegrass, and rock, yet she honors those genres by tapping into their most emotionally stirring qualities. She began achieving hits while in California, appealing to rock and country crowds, and after moving to Nashville and onto the country charts, she continued to experiment and to attract diverse audiences.

STATLER BROTHERS

Formed 1961 in Staunton, Virginia

The Statler Brothers presented a combination of musical talent, showmanship, and humor, creating a career that lasted more than half a century. Influenced by gospel quartets, the vocal group included Harold Reid, his brother Don Reid, Phil Balsley, and Lew Dewitt. Health issues led Dewitt to leave in 1982, replaced by Jimmy Fortune.

Tom T. Hall at the 2008 Medallion Ceremony.

ERNEST V. "POP" STONEMAN

b. May 25, 1893; d. June 14, 1968 • Monarat, Virginia

Patriarch of a legendary musical family, Pop Stoneman helped establish country music's validity during its first wave of commercial success. He hit as early as 1925, recording event songs, sentimental tunes, and gospel standards. The Great Depression ended his early career, but he returned after World War II leading his children in the Stoneman Family band.

2009

ROY CLARK

b. April 15, 1933 • Meherrin, Virginia

An all-around entertainer, Roy Clark is a vocalist and master guitarist whose range as a showman has included playing a pickin' and grinnin' bumpkin on TV and in movies as well as performing with symphony orchestras; headlining in Las Vegas; running his own theater in Branson, Missouri; and being a recurring fill-in host on *The Tonight Show*.

BARBARA MANDRELL

b. December 15, 1948 • Houston, Texas

Few entertainers have been as hard-working or as multi-talented as Barbara Mandrell. A seasoned pro who could play several instruments by age fourteen, she was a hit recording artist at twenty-one. She went on to star on network television as host of a variety show and to headline in Las Vegas.

CHARLIE McCOY

b. March 28, 1941 • Oak Hill, West Virginia

The most recorded harmonica player in history, Charlie McCoy has graced the recordings of artists ranging from Elvis Presley and Bob Dylan to George Jones and Loretta Lynn. His musicianship is distinguished by its speed, precision, clarity, phrasing, and emotional depth. McCoy is almost single-handedly responsible for re-establishing the harmonica as a popular instrument in country music.

2010

JIMMY DEAN

b. August 10, 1928; d. June 13, 2010 • Olton, Texas

Jimmy Dean's affable charm and fresh-faced looks epitomized the country TV star of the 1950s. Though Dean was able to parlay his specialty, the dramatic narrative, into a string of hit records in the 1960s, he gained his biggest success as the host of televised variety shows, as a fill-in host of network talk shows, and as an actor in TV and film.

FERLIN HUSKY

b. December 3, 1925; d. March 17, 2011 • Cantwell, Missouri

Entertainer extraordinare Ferlin Husky started in Southern California as a radio host, a television regular, a country hit-maker, and a humorist who performed under his alter-ego Simon Crum. By 1956, Husky recorded in Music City, with his 1957 hit "Gone" credited as the beginning of the polished Nashville Sound. He continued to chart hits into the 1970s.

BILLY SHERRILL

b. November 5, 1936 • Phil Campbell, Alabama

One of the most influential producers in history, Billy Sherrill helped shape the evolving sound of country music, especially in the 1970s. Every artist he worked with prospered under his visionary direction, including George Jones, Tammy Wynette, Charlie Rich, Tanya Tucker, Barbara Mandrell, David Houston, and Johnny Paycheck.

2011

BOBBY BRADDOCK

b. August 5, 1940 • Lakeland, Florida

One of Nashville's most admired and inventive songwriters, Bobby Braddock landed his first cut in 1966 and eventually penned such country classics as Tammy Wynette's "D-I-V-O-R-C-E" and George Jones's "He Stopped Loving Her Today," both cowritten with Curly Putman. Decades later, Braddock had hits with Tracy Lawrence, Toby Keith, and Billy Currington.

112

REBA McENTIRE
b. March 28, 1955 • McAlester, Oklahoma

Reba McEntire is the most successful female performer of her generation, and she has been cited as a role model by nearly every female country singer to follow. She has had more #1 country albums than any female singer in history, and she also succeeded as an author, a businesswoman, and an actor on Broadway, on film, and on TV.

JEAN SHEPARD
b. November 1, 1933 • Pauls Valley, Oklahoma

Jean Shepard was one of the few women to become country stars in the 1950s, and even rarer, she did so with feisty honky-tonk songs and candid material. Her lively style set the stage for the breakthroughs of Loretta Lynn, Dolly Parton, and Tammy Wynette, and she continued to gain hit records into the 1970s.

2012

GARTH BROOKS
b. February 7, 1962 • Luba, Oklahoma

Garth Brooks emerged in the 1990s to become one of the biggest-selling music acts of all time. In the process, he helped move country into the mainstream of American entertainment. After selling more than 100 million albums, he announced his retirement in 2000 to raise his children. He since has staged periodic concerts and occasionally released new records without fully resuming his career.

HARGUS "PIG" ROBBINS
b. January 18, 1938 • Rhea County, Tennessee

Blind pianist Pig Robbins succeeded Floyd Cramer as the leading session keyboardist in Nashville, from the mid-1960s through the 1980s. Robbins's first hit session yielded George Jones's "White Lightning," and he went on to record with everyone from Bob Dylan and Neil Young to Crystal Gayle, Charlie Rich, Randy Travis, and Alan Jackson.

Ferlin Husky and Charley Pride at the 2010 Medallion Ceremony.

CONNIE SMITH
b. August 14, 1941 • Elkhart, Indiana

Connie Smith shot to stardom with her first release, the #1 hit "Once a Day." Her expressive voice offered a matchless combination of tone, power, phrasing, and emotion, but her greatness extends beyond vocal brilliance. It encompasses her song selection, her connection to great musicians, her classy demeanor, and a spiritual bearing that serves as her foundation. ■